ZIC ACK Neu

1

ASSESSMENT SUPPORT PACK

TEACHER'S NOTES

Judy Somerville

Nelson

Thomas Nelson and Sons Ltd
Nelson House Mayfield Road
Walton-on-Thames Surrey
KT12 5PL UK

First published by Thomas Nelson and Sons Ltd 1993

I(T)P® Thomas Nelson is an International
Thomson Publishing Company

I(T)P® is used under licence

ISBN 0-17-439794-1
NPN 9 8 7 6 5 4

Printed in China

Acknowledgements

Illustration:
David Birdsall
Phillip Burrows
Lucie Richmond
Stan Stevens
Nancy Sutcliffe
Charles Whelon

Contents

Zickzack neu Assessment Support Pack

Introduction

This Assessment Support Pack provides comprehensive guidance and materials to enable teachers and students to assess progress throughout Stage 1 of **Zickzack neu**. The pack consists of
- One set of Copymasters
- One set of Teacher's Notes
- One Master Cassette.

The Copymasters provide
- 10 end-of-chapter tests
- 1 set of cumulative tests
- solutions to all tests
- student and teacher record sheets.

The Teacher's Notes provide
- detailed guidance on formative and summative assessment
- miniature versions of summative test material
- transcripts of all recorded material
- solutions to all tests, including suggested points totals for test items
- an indication of the National Curriculum Levels of the test items.

The Master Cassette provides
- material for listening tests
- models for speaking tests.

Formative and summative assessment

As learners ourselves, in whatever field, we are constantly attempting to evaluate and assess our performance, to pinpoint information about the progress we are making towards our intended goals. The information we gather, from other learners and from teachers or instructors, is vital if we are to improve upon our performance and continue to make significant progress. It is in this sense that both continuous assessment of everyday activities and more formal tests are an integral part of the learning process: they help to stimulate effective learning and teaching. However, there is a clear distinction between these two types of assessment.

a) Formative assessment

Broadly speaking, formative assessment is a continuous process which provides information to help students and teachers gauge progress. Quite simply, it consists of observing, commenting on and recording students' progress during everyday classroom activities, a logical extension of what occurs in Modern Language lessons already.

b) Summative assessment

As its names implies, summative assessment marks an end point, a summary of what students have apparently been able to achieve within a defined period of time. Such assessment usually takes the form of end-of-unit tests, end-of-year examinations or public examinations.

Motivation and threat

There can be no doubt that we all feel threatened by summative assessment. It is seen as a one-and-only chance to prove that we have made the grade, and it is generally conducted in daunting examination conditions. Students face such tests with anxiety about possible tricky or even unfair questions and with a dread of failure, which is never to be mitigated by the conviction that they performed well all year or all term.

Summative assessment has a rightful place alongside formative assessment, in that it serves to confirm what is already known to both students and teachers. Formative assessment helps to provide this 'prior knowledge'. It is, quite simply, feedback from teachers and others which gives students the opportunity to capitalise on their strengths, to recognise and address weak points and to try again. This is the essence of formative assessment, which, by its very nature, is non-threatening and potentially highly motivating.

It is on this basis that the **Zickzack neu** Assessment Support Pack has been written: with formative assessment, appropriately recorded, providing a reservoir of detailed information on the learner's performance throughout, and with summative tests, representing a periodic dipstick into this reservoir, providing a sample to confirm the results already registered through observation.

The combined information deriving from the two forms of assessment is invaluable to a whole host of interested parties, from learners to teachers, parents/guardians, governors, examination groups, employers, education authorities and the government.

Formative assessment

Opportunities for assessment

It is crucial to the process of assessment that teachers exercise their professional judgement in all matters relating to levels of student performance.

For the purposes of formative assessment, teachers will find it invaluable to refer to the Overview in the introduction to the **Zickzack neu** Stage 1 Teacher's Book. This lists all the activities for each chapter of **Zickzack neu** Stage 1 with the National Curriculum Level suggested by each activity.

The Overview gives clear definition to the levels within which classes using **Zickzack neu** Stage 1 are likely to be operating (largely levels 1 to 3 throughout, with numerous instances of Level 4). This definition should help teachers and students to concentrate on a relatively narrow range of attainment. Nevertheless, there must always be scope for individuals who fall outside this range. In practice, much of the additional evidence for such students will come from the differentiated materials in Stage 1 of **Zickzack neu**.

In order to make use of this information for formative assessment, teachers may find it helpful to follow these steps:

1 Become familiar with the national criteria for assessment;
2 Familiarise students with the criteria;
3 Select students who seem ready for assessment;
4 Select activities for assessment using the Overview in the Teacher's Book;
5 Plan the organisation of the lesson so that the teacher is free to observe;
6 Observe students and provide feedback;
7 Either record results or identify with students any shortcomings and agree appropriate action.

Familiarisation with national criteria

It is of equal importance that not only teachers but also their students understand and have access to the national criteria: unless students know what their objectives are, they can hardly be expected to understand and use the information they receive from assessment.

Besides, students can and must take an active role in assessment if a full picture of their performance is to emerge. Students are increasingly expected to work more independently and to exercise choice, express opinions and evaluate their work.

Zickzack neu provides ample opportunities for autonomous learning: for example, with the *Selbstbedienung* sections of the Students' Book, in some Copymaster activities, the Activity Cards and the software programs. Students following the course will, therefore, be used to choosing and marking their own work.

Teachers and students may also be familiar with the *Personalakte* Copymasters (also included among the Assessment Support Pack Copymasters) which provide information on students' attitudes and reactions to activities they have completed. This information helps students and teachers to diagnose weaknesses and celebrate strengths and, thereby, to identify ways in which students can improve their performance.

Consequently, it is both desirable and necessary to involve students fully in the assessment process.

Selecting students and activities for assessment

Clearly it is neither necessary nor helpful to attempt to assess every student in the same activities at the same time. Firstly, time does not permit this; secondly, different students progress at different rates; and thirdly, as the Overview in the Stage 1 Teacher's Book demonstrates, there are numerous activities at each level throughout **Zickzack neu** Stage 1 which can be used for assessment.

Observation of student performance and on-the-spot feedback are essential ingredients in a successful learning programme. In many cases this will not lead to formally recording student performance: teachers who assess everything run the risk of intimidating and demotivating students. On the other hand, students do need regular praise, encouragement and guidance as to how and what they need to improve. What the teacher gains at this point is informal information which helps to build up a substantial impression of student performance.

Once students' readiness for assessment has become apparent through their work in class or through homework assignments, it is advisable to assess them as soon as possible, selecting appropriate activities from the Overview. Bearing in mind the need to observe and assess small numbers of students at any one time, lessons will have to be structured in such a way as to ensure enough free time for the teacher to carry out the assessments.

Structuring lessons for independent work and assessment

In order to free themselves to carry out assessment, teachers may wish to consider the following:

- stage reached within the unit: teacher input not required;
- length of time available in relation to the assessment activities selected;
- maximum number of students to be assessed at any one time;
- suitability of the room and its layout for independent work;
- students' familiarity with and access to equipment and materials (including solutions, transcripts and reference sources);
- availability of support, e.g. Foreign Language Assistant, other staff, parents, older students.

Observing, providing feedback and recording

Students will have to perform at any given level on a number of occasions and over a period of time. Therefore it is likely that students will need to record performances at the same level more than once.

Having observed a small group of students performing a chosen activity, the teacher will wish to:

- discuss with students their level of performance;
- decide with each student whether or not to record the results on the Student Record Chart (included among the Assessment Support Pack Copymasters);
- give appropriate advice for the next assessment, at the same or a higher level.

The Student Record Chart

Students should enter the title of the activity and the date on the Record Chart, having agreed with the teacher the appropriate entry. These details should then be initialled by the teacher. The Record Charts should remain in school but are the property of students.

The details shown on the Student Record Chart will be supplemented by information collated in the teacher's markbook on other classwork activities and homework assignments. Teachers may well wish to give students the opportunity to transfer information about homework assignments from the teacher's markbook to the Student Record Chart. Each student's chart will be unique in that it will not necessarily have the same entries as those of other students in the class.

Example of an entry on a Student Record Chart

RECORD CHART

Name: Sharon Smith Klasse: 7CB

HÖ = HÖREN SP = SPRECHEN L = LESEN SCH = SCHREIBEN

ÜBUNG	QUELLE	NIVEAU(S)	DATUM	LEHRER(IN)
1 Fotoquiz	SB Kapitel 1	HÖ 1 SP 2 LE 2	1. Okt. 1993	CAB

Markbooks should also conform to the criteria and show the title and source of activities and levels attained in the respective skill areas.

Example of a teacher's markbook entry

	Was läuft? SB, Kap. 1 (ATs 1, 2, 3)	
Sharon Smith	AT1 2 AT2 1 AT3 1	

Evidence of students' assessed work should also be retained for the purposes of moderation. One such example could be a portfolio of work, including a student cassette of speaking activities.

The software which accompanies **Zickzack neu**, the *Zickzack neu Textfiles* also provides a wide variety of activities, some of which teachers may wish to use for formative assessment purposes. Information Technology Co-ordinators may wish to discuss with Modern Language teachers the possibility of delivering aspects of the IT National Curriculum requirements through Modern Languages.

Summative Assessment

Format of the end-of-chapter tests

There are ten end-of-chapter tests, plus a cumulative test (*Abschlußtest*) for use at the end of the year.

The tests are divided by skill area (**Hören, Sprechen, Lesen, Schreiben**) and the emphasis for marking purposes is placed upon the named skill area in each case. Wherever possible, however, test activities involve the use of more than one skill. The emphasis, therefore, is on single-skill testing in mixed-skill contexts.

Level of difficulty

The test activities for each skill area are presented in ascending order of difficulty. In the Stage 1 Assessment Support Pack the majority of the test activities, like the activities in the core materials, are pitched at levels 1 to 3 of the National Curriculum, with a number of more open-ended activities, particularly in the later tests, pitched at levels 4 or 5.

The National Curriculum Level of each activity is indicated both below the solutions in these Teacher's Notes and alongside the miniature versions of the Copymasters, also reproduced in the Teacher's Notes. Where a mixed-skill task is involved, appropriate levels are given for each Attainment Target. Where a task is more open-ended in nature, an appropriate range of levels is given.

The levels given are those suggested by the language involved and the activity type. It is possible, by withdrawing support (for example, lists of words/phrases for gap-filling activities) or by giving extra help (for example, lists of words/phrases for writing tasks), to alter the level of some activities. Here, as always, the professional judgement of the teacher is crucial in assessing the student's level of performance.

Although teachers will probably wish to make sure that their students have learnt the key language items for each unit of **Zickzack neu** Stage 1 and will, therefore, want students to complete the majority of these items for each chapter, flexibility is provided by the fact that, in some cases, there is more than one test item at the same level. It is therefore not necessary to use all the test items. This may help particularly when time is at a premium.

Equally, allowing for differentiation of attainment, not all students will necessarily be able to complete all the activities for each skill area in a particular chapter.

Rubrics and glossaries

In line with the **Zickzack neu** core materials and national criteria, all the instructions for the summative test items are given in German. These are supported by a glossary at the foot of each Copymaster, where instructions are translated into English. The purpose of this glossary is to help students understand the activities without necessarily seeking assistance from the teacher. If the teacher wishes, this support can be removed by folding back or cutting off the bottom of each Copymaster, as indicated by the scissor line.

Conducting reading and writing tests

The tests relating to reading and writing are designed to be conducted swiftly and efficiently within the context of normal lessons and usually within about 20 to 25 minutes. As indicated earlier, wherever possible test items have a mixed-skill context. Therefore, one writing test item also involves listening to material on the cassette.

Listening tests

The listening tests are also designed to be completed comfortably within a single lesson. The cassette provided is a duplicating master. This allows schools to make multiple copies of the cassette for teachers and for students and provides the flexibility for students to complete the listening tests in a number of ways: for example on an individual or small group basis, with the whole class using headsets or with the teacher controlling the cassette player.

Speaking tests

The teacher is not expected to conduct individual speaking tests with every student in the class. There is ample scope here for Foreign Language Assistants, team teachers and parents voluntarily involved in classroom activities to assist in the assessment of speaking activities.

Peer assessment, usually on a pairwork basis, can also save teachers a great deal of time and play an important part in motivating students and involving them in the assessment process. Students could gain valuable training for this during the formative assessment process, where the teacher is available to observe students working together and encourage them to assess one another. It is also possible to appoint a third student to observe and assess a pair. Solutions to the test activities for each skill, together with suggested points totals, are included in the Assessment Support Pack Copymasters, for students to use in assessing themselves and/or one another, where teachers so wish.

A cassette version of the speaking tests is provided to help any students who experience difficulties when preparing for these tests. Teachers can copy the appropriate item(s) on cassette for students to take away and prepare, either at home or independently in class.

As in formative assessment, students may wish to make a cassette recording of their performance in speaking tests, as evidence of their attainment.

Marking and points system

A points total for each test item has been included to provide a quick guide to student performance and to assist the teacher in weighing up whether or not the tests bear out the evidence of formative assessment.

This is not intended, however, to replace assessment by national criteria. Teachers are still expected to use their professional judgement in applying those criteria to student performances, rather than producing a formula to convert raw points into levels. No such formula exists and conversion charts are unlikely to be produced or promoted under the National Curriculum.

The Annual Summary Chart

The Annual Summary Chart (included among the Assessment Support Pack Copymasters) should be completed at the end of the year for handover to the next teacher and for use in planning meetings and discussions about moderation. For each of the four skill areas (corresponding to National Curriculum Attainment Targets) all ten levels of attainment are shown. There are two lines for each skill area: one for class activities which have been used in formative assessment and the other for summative test results. Teachers can use the suggested colour-coding to chart students' progress for up to five years of secondary education. The code suggested is:

red	for year 7
orange	for year 8
yellow	for year 9
green	for year 10
blue	for year 11

Teachers can then colour the four skill areas like bar graphs, stopping at the furthest point within each skill area achieved in a single school year. This will enable teachers and other interested parties (for example, parents and governors) to see at a glance the kind of progress students have been able to make from one year to the next. It may well assist in the planning of future teaching programmes and activities.

An example of an Annual Summary Chart entry is shown on page 8.

Moderation and standardisation

Departments should agree on their marking and assessment policy, in the light of national criteria, and build into their scheme moderation meetings, during which samples of assessed work are discussed and compared, to ensure consistency across the department. Students should be able to agree with their teachers the level of their attainment shown by completed activities. In cases where there are discrepancies between expected and actual test results, students and teachers will need to review the student's overall performance and identify an appropriate programme of revision and consolidation. This is likely to involve reference to the *Tip des Tages* and *Auf einen Blick* sections in the Students' Book and to the *Grammatik Überblick* grammar reference section and its related consolidation activities on Copymasters, as well as work from the Activity Box and using software.

Example of an entry on an Annual Summary Chart

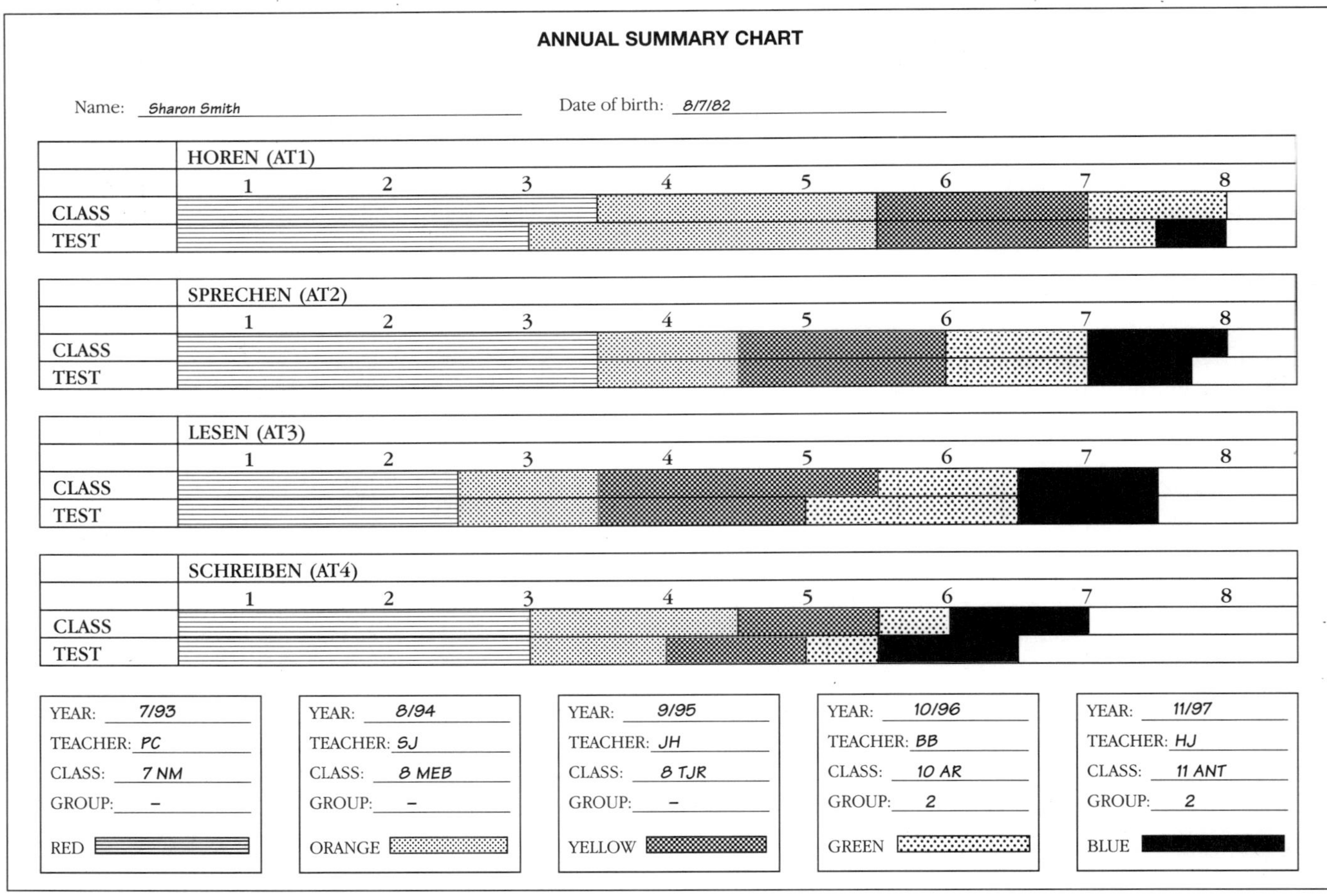

Summative test material

KAPITEL 1

AT1 1
AT3 1
AT4 1

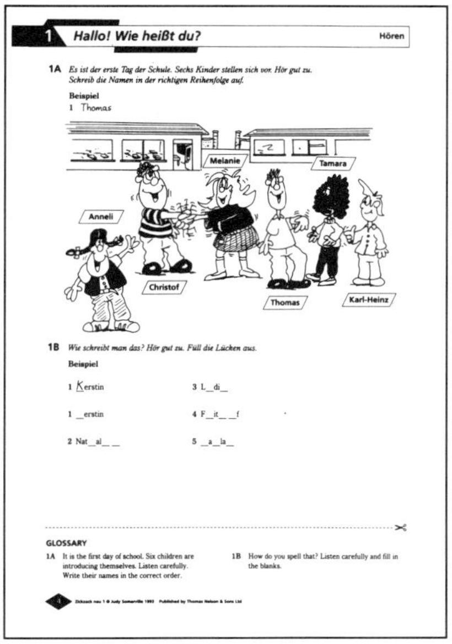

1 **Hallo! Wie heißt du?** Hören

1A *Es ist der erste Tag der Schule. Sechs Kinder stellen sich vor. Hör gut zu. Schreib die Namen in der richtigen Reihenfolge auf.*

Beispiel
1 Thomas

AT1 1

1B *Wie schreibt man das? Hör gut zu. Füll die Lücken aus.*

Beispiel

1 Kerstin
1 _erstin
2 Nat_al_ _
3 L_di_
4 F_it_ _f
5 _a_la_

GLOSSARY

1A It is the first day of school. Six children are introducing themselves. Listen carefully. Write their names in the correct order.

1B How do you spell that? Listen carefully and fill in the blanks.

AT1 1

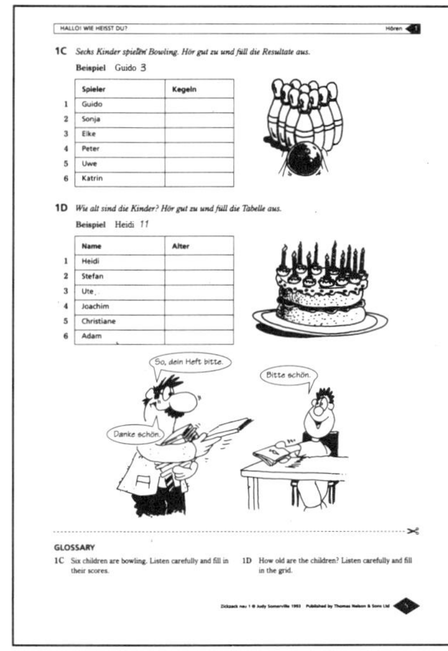

HALLO! WIE HEISST DU? Hören

1C *Sechs Kinder spielen Bowling. Hör gut zu und füll die Resultate aus.*

Beispiel Guido 3

	Spieler	Kegeln
1	Guido	
2	Sonja	
3	Elke	
4	Peter	
5	Uwe	
6	Katrin	

AT1 2

1D *Wie alt sind die Kinder? Hör gut zu und füll die Tabelle aus.*

Beispiel Heidi 11

	Name	Alter
1	Heidi	
2	Stefan	
3	Ute	
4	Joachim	
5	Christiane	
6	Adam	

GLOSSARY

1C Six children are bowling. Listen carefully and fill in their scores.

1D How old are the children? Listen carefully and fill in the grid.

AT2 1

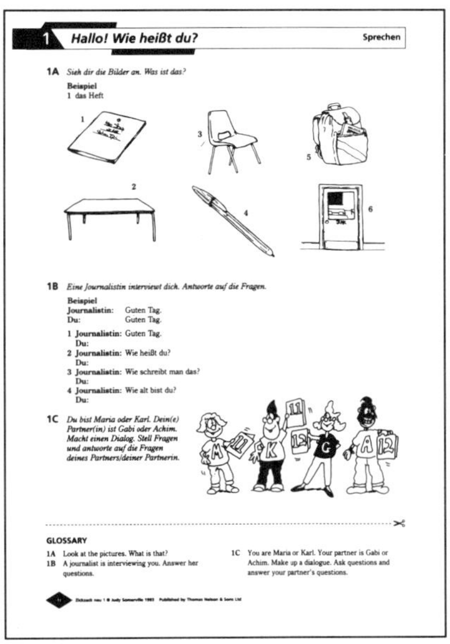

1 **Hallo! Wie heißt du?** Sprechen

1A *Sieh dir die Bilder an. Was ist das?*

Beispiel
1 das Heft

1 2 3 4 5 6

AT2 2
AT1 2

1B *Eine Journalistin interviewt dich. Antworte auf die Fragen.*

Beispiel
Journalistin: Guten Tag.
Du: Guten Tag.

1 **Journalistin:** Guten Tag.
Du:
2 **Journalistin:** Wie heißt du?
Du:
3 **Journalistin:** Wie schreibt man das?
Du:
4 **Journalistin:** Wie alt bist du?
Du:

AT2 2

1C *Du bist Maria oder Karl. Dein(e) Partner(in) ist Gabi oder Achim. Macht einen Dialog. Stell Fragen und antworte auf die Fragen deines Partners/deiner Partnerin.*

GLOSSARY

1A Look at the pictures. What is that?

1B A journalist is interviewing you. Answer her questions.

1C You are Maria or Karl. Your partner is Gabi or Achim. Make up a dialogue. Ask questions and answer your partner's questions.

AT3 1

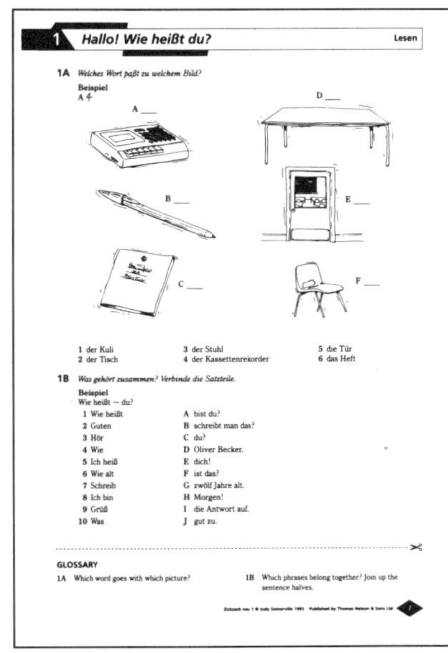

1 **Hallo! Wie heißt du?** Lesen

1A *Welches Wort paßt zu welchem Bild?*

Beispiel
A 4

A ___ B ___ C ___ D ___ E ___ F ___

1 der Kuli
2 der Tisch
3 der Stuhl
4 der Kassettenrekorder
5 die Tür
6 das Heft

AT3 2

1B *Was gehört zusammen? Verbinde die Satzteile.*

Beispiel
Wie heißt – du?

1 Wie heißt	A bist du?
2 Guten	B schreibt man das?
3 Hör	C du?
4 Wie	D Oliver Becker.
5 Ich heiß	E dich!
6 Wie alt	F ist das?
7 Schreib	G zwölf Jahre alt.
8 Ich bin	H Morgen!
9 Grüß	I die Antwort auf.
10 Was	J gut zu.

GLOSSARY

1A Which word goes with which picture?

1B Which phrases belong together? Join up the sentence halves.

AT3 2

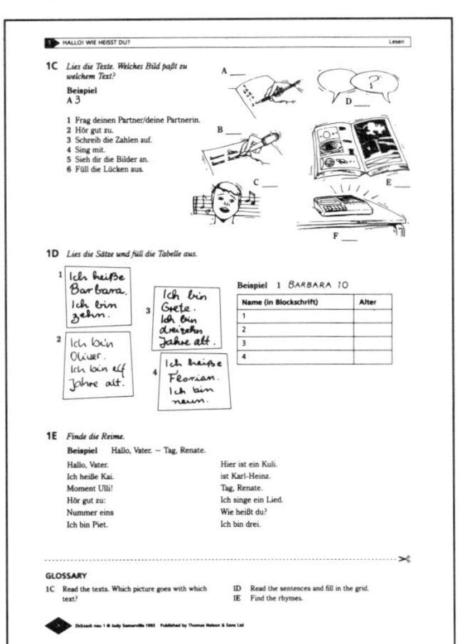

HALLO! WIE HEISST DU? Lesen

1C *Lies die Texte. Welches Bild paßt zu welchem Text?*

Beispiel
A 3

1 Frag deinen Partner/deine Partnerin.
2 Hör gut zu.
3 Schreib die Zahlen auf.
4 Sing mit.
5 Sieh dir die Bilder an.
6 Füll die Lücken aus.

A ___ B ___ C ___ D ___ E ___ F ___

AT3 2
AT4 1

1D *Lies die Sätze und füll die Tabelle aus.*

1 Ich heiße Barbara. Ich bin zehn.
2 Ich bin Oliver. Ich bin elf Jahre alt.
3 Ich bin Grete. Ich bin dreizehn Jahre alt.
4 Ich heiße Florian. Ich bin neun.

Beispiel 1 BARBARA 10

Name (in Blockschrift)	Alter
1	
2	
3	
4	

AT3 2

1E *Finde die Reime.*

Beispiel Hallo, Vater. ~ Tag, Renate.

Hallo, Vater.	Hier ist ein Kuli.
Ich heiße Kai.	ist Karl-Heinz.
Moment Ulli!	Tag, Renate.
Hör gut zu:	Ich singe ein Lied.
Nummer eins	Wie heißt du?
Ich bin Piet.	Ich bin drei.

GLOSSARY

1C Read the texts. Which picture goes with which text?

1D Read the sentences and fill in the grid.

1E Find the rhymes.

AT4 1

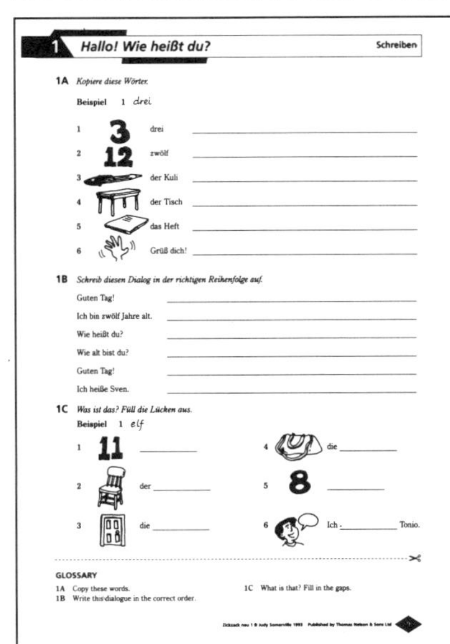

1 **Hallo! Wie heißt du?** Schreiben

1A *Kopiere diese Wörter.*

Beispiel 1 drei

1 3 drei ______
2 12 zwölf ______
3 der Kuli ______
4 der Tisch ______
5 das Heft ______
6 Grüß dich! ______

AT4 2
AT3 2

1B *Schreib diesen Dialog in der richtigen Reihenfolge auf.*

Guten Tag! ______
Ich bin zwölf Jahre alt. ______
Wie heißt du? ______
Wie alt bist du? ______
Guten Tag! ______
Ich heiße Sven. ______

AT4 2

1C *Was ist das? Füll die Lücken aus.*

Beispiel 1 elf

1 11 ______
2 der ______
3 die ______
4 die ______
5 8 ______
6 Ich ______ Tonio.

GLOSSARY

1A Copy these words.

1B Write this dialogue in the correct order.

1C What is that? Fill in the gaps.

KAPITEL 2

AT1 1
AT3 1

AT1 2
AT3 1

AT1 2
AT3 1

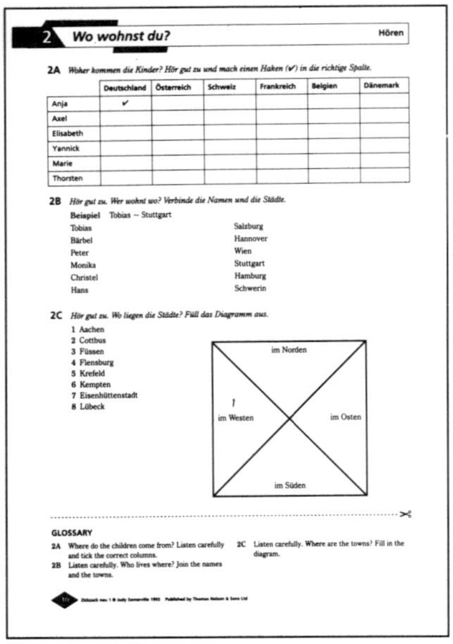
2 Wo wohnst du? Hören

2A Woher kommen die Kinder? Hör gut zu und mach einen Haken (✔) in die richtige Spalte.

	Deutschland	Österreich	Schweiz	Frankreich	Belgien	Dänemark
Anja	✔					
Axel						
Elisabeth						
Yannick						
Marie						
Thorsten						

2B Hör gut zu. Wer wohnt wo? Verbinde die Namen und die Städte.
Beispiel Tobias – Stuttgart

Tobias	Salzburg
Bärbel	Hannover
Peter	Wien
Monika	Stuttgart
Christel	Hamburg
Hans	Schwerin

2C Hör gut zu. Wo liegen die Städte? Füll das Diagramm aus.
1 Aachen
2 Cottbus
3 Füssen
4 Flensburg
5 Krefeld
6 Kempten
7 Eisenhüttenstadt
8 Lübeck

GLOSSARY
2A Where do the children come from? Listen carefully and tick the correct columns.
2B Listen carefully. Who lives where? Join the names and the towns.
2C Listen carefully. Where are the towns? Fill in the diagram.

AT2 1

AT2 2
AT3 1

AT2 2
AT3 2

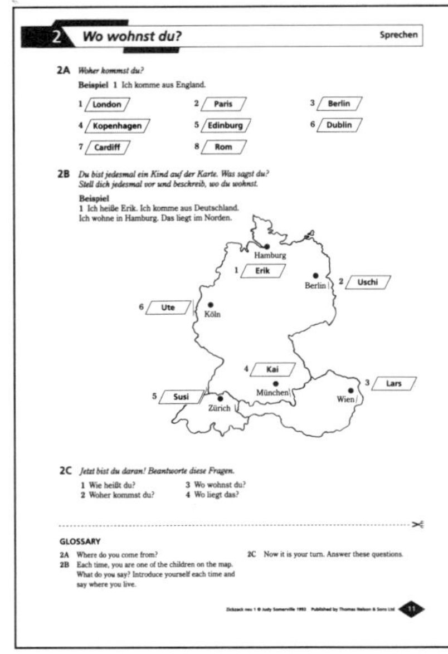
2 Wo wohnst du? Sprechen

2A Woher kommst du?
Beispiel 1 Ich komme aus England.
1 London 2 Paris 3 Berlin
4 Kopenhagen 5 Edinburg 6 Dublin
7 Cardiff 8 Rom

2B Du bist jedesmal ein Kind auf der Karte. Was sagst du? Stell dich jedesmal vor und beschreib, wo du wohnst.
Beispiel
1 Ich heiße Erik. Ich komme aus Deutschland.
Ich wohne in Hamburg. Das liegt im Norden.

2C Jetzt bist du daran! Beantworte diese Fragen.
1 Wie heißt du? 3 Wo wohnst du?
2 Woher kommst du? 4 Wo liegt das?

GLOSSARY
2A Where do you come from?
2B Each time, you are one of the children on the map. What do you say? Introduce yourself each time and say where you live.
2C Now it is your turn. Answer these questions.

AT3 1

AT3 2

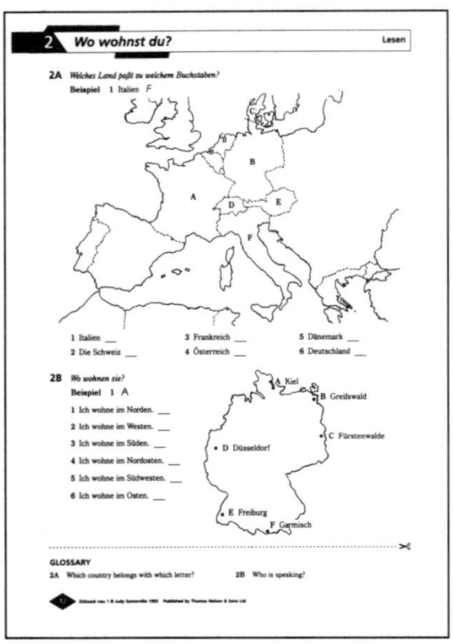
2 Wo wohnst du? Lesen

2A Welches Land paßt zu welchem Buchstaben?
Beispiel 1 Italien F

1 Italien ___ 3 Frankreich ___ 5 Dänemark ___
2 Die Schweiz ___ 4 Österreich ___ 6 Deutschland ___

2B Wo wohnen sie?
Beispiel 1 A
1 Ich wohne im Norden. ___
2 Ich wohne im Westen. ___
3 Ich wohne im Süden. ___
4 Ich wohne im Nordosten. ___
5 Ich wohne im Südwesten. ___
6 Ich wohne im Osten. ___

GLOSSARY
2A Which country belongs with which letter?
2B Who is speaking?

AT3 2

AT3 2

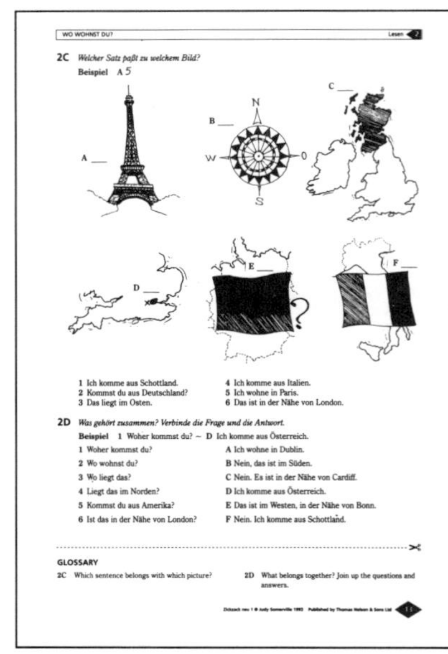
WO WOHNST DU? Lesen 2

2C Welcher Satz paßt zu welchem Bild?
Beispiel A 5

1 Ich komme aus Schottland.
2 Kommst du aus Deutschland?
3 Das liegt im Osten.
4 Ich komme aus Italien.
5 Ich wohne in Paris.
6 Das ist in der Nähe von London.

2D Was gehört zusammen? Verbinde die Frage und die Antwort.
Beispiel 1 Woher kommst du? – D Ich komme aus Österreich.
1 Woher kommst du?
2 Wo wohnst du?
3 Wo liegt das?
4 Liegt das im Norden?
5 Kommst du aus Amerika?
6 Ist das in der Nähe von London?
A Ich wohne in Dublin.
B Nein, das ist im Süden.
C Nein. Es ist in der Nähe von Cardiff.
D Ich komme aus Österreich.
E Das ist im Westen, in der Nähe von Bonn.
F Nein. Ich komme aus Schottland.

GLOSSARY
2C Which sentence belongs with which picture?
2D What belongs together? Join up the questions and answers.

AT4 1
AT3 1

AT4 2
AT3 2

AT4 2
AT3 2

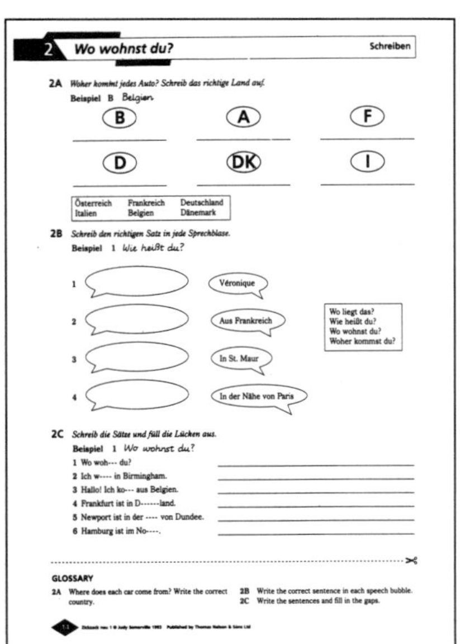
2 Wo wohnst du? Schreiben

2A Woher kommt jedes Auto? Schreib das richtige Land auf.
Beispiel B Belgien
B A F
D DK I

Österreich Frankreich Deutschland
Italien Belgien Dänemark

2B Schreib den richtigen Satz in jede Sprechblase.
Beispiel 1 Wie heißt du?
1 Véronique
2 Aus Frankreich
3 In St. Maur
4 In der Nähe von Paris

Wo liegt das?
Wie heißt du?
Wo wohnst du?
Woher kommst du?

2C Schreib die Sätze und füll die Lücken aus.
Beispiel 1 Wo wohnst du?
1 Wo woh--- du?
2 Ich w---- in Birmingham.
3 Hallo! Ich ko--- aus Belgien.
4 Frankfurt ist in D-----land.
5 Newport ist in der ---- von Dundee.
6 Hamburg ist im No----.

GLOSSARY
2A Where does each car come from? Write the correct country.
2B Write the correct sentence in each speech bubble.
2C Write the sentences and fill in the gaps.

KAPITEL 3

AT1 1

AT1 2

AT1 2
AT3 1

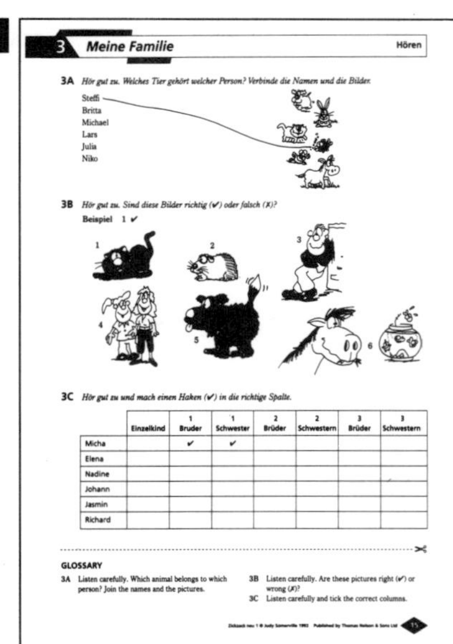
3 Meine Familie Hören

3A Hör gut zu. Welches Tier gehört welcher Person? Verbinde die Namen und die Bilder.
Steffi
Britta
Michael
Lars
Julia
Niko

3B Hör gut zu. Sind diese Bilder richtig (✔) oder falsch (✗)?
Beispiel 1 ✔

3C Hör gut zu und mach einen Haken (✔) in die richtige Spalte.

	Einzelkind	1 Bruder	1 Schwester	2 Brüder	2 Schwestern	3 Brüder	3 Schwestern
Micha		✔	✔				
Elena							
Nadine							
Johann							
Jasmin							
Richard							

GLOSSARY
3A Listen carefully. Which animal belongs to which person? Join the names and the pictures.
3B Listen carefully. Are these pictures right (✔) or wrong (✗)?
3C Listen carefully and tick the correct columns.

AT2 1

AT2 2

3 Meine Familie — Sprechen

3A *Was ist das?*

Beispiel
1 A: Was ist das?
B: Das ist ein Hund.

3B *Was sagst du?*
Stell dich jedesmal vor und beschreib die Fotos.

Beispiel 1 Ich heiße Paul. Ich habe eine Schwester.

Jetzt bist du daran! Beschreib dich.

GLOSSARY
3A What is that?
3B What do you say? Introduce yourself each time and describe the photos. Now it is your turn! Describe yourself.

16 Zickzack neu 1 © Judy Somerville 1993 Published by Thomas Nelson & Sons Ltd

AT2 2
AT3 2

AT2 2,3
AT1 2
AT3 1

MEINE FAMILIE — Sprechen 3

3C *Hier sind die Antworten.*
Was waren die Fragen?

1 Ich heiße Susanne.
2 Ich wohne in Wien.
3 Ich bin zwölf Jahre alt.
4 Nein. Ich bin ein Einzelkind.
5 Ja. Ich habe ein Meerschweinchen.

3D *Mach ein Interview mit einem Partner/einer Partnerin und füll dieses Formular aus.*

Mein Partner/Meine Partnerin

Name: ______________________

Alter: ______________________

Geschwister: ______________________

____

____

Haustiere: ______________________

____

____

Beantworte dann die Fragen deines Partners/deiner Partnerin.

GLOSSARY
3C Here are the answers. What were the questions?
3D Interview your partner and fill in this form. Then answer your partner's questions.

Zickzack neu 1 © Judy Somerville 1993 Published by Thomas Nelson & Sons Ltd 17

AT3 1

AT3 2

3 Meine Familie — Lesen

3A *Was ist das? Unterstreich die richtigen Wörter.*

Beispiel

1	der Hund	die Katze	das Kaninchen
1	der Hund	die Katze	das Kaninchen
2	der Hamster	die Maus	das Meerschweinchen
3	der Vogel	die Ratte	das Pferd
4	der Hund	die Wüstenmaus	das Kaninchen
5	die Schlange	das Kaninchen	das Meerschweinchen
6	der Hund	die Schlange	das Kaninchen

3B *Welches Bild paßt zu welchem Text?*

Beispiel A 3

1 Ich heiße Sascha. Ich bin zwölf Jahre alt. Ich habe eine Schwester und einen Bruder.
2 Ich heiße Miriam. Ich habe zwei Brüder. Sie sind sieben und neun.
3 Ich heiße Rainer. Ich habe eine Schwester. Sie ist drei Jahre alt.
4 Ich heiße Lisa. Mein Bruder ist zwei Jahre alt. Er heißt Dieter.
5 Ich bin Jörg. Ich habe drei Schwestern.
6 Ich heiße Peter. Ich habe zwei Schwestern, Trudi und Anna.

GLOSSARY
3A What is that? Underline the correct words.
3B Which picture goes with which text?

18 Zickzack neu 1 © Judy Somerville 1993 Published by Thomas Nelson & Sons Ltd

AT3 2

AT3 3
AT4 1

MEINE FAMILIE — Lesen 3

3C *Welches Wort fehlt?*

Beispiel 1 C

1 Ich habe eine Schwester.
Sie ____________ Carola.
2 Ich habe zwei ____________:
einen Bruder und eine Schwester.
3 Ich habe einen ____________ und
zwei Kaninchen.
4 Ich bin ____________. Ich habe keine
Geschwister.
5 Ich habe drei ____________: Andreas,
Peter und Alexander.

A Hund
B Brüder
C heißt
D Einzelkind
E Geschwister

3D *Lies die Postkarte und die Sätze. Welche Sätze sind richtig und welche sind falsch?*

Beispiel 1 richtig

Lieber James!
Ich bin Dein neuer Brieffreund.
Ich heiße Udo, und ich bin zwölf
Jahre alt. Ich habe einen Bruder
und eine Schwester. Mein Bruder
heißt Tobias, und meine
Schwester heißt Karin. Tobias
ist acht Jahre alt, und Karin ist
zehn. Ich habe eine Katze, und
meine Geschwister haben zwei
Kaninchen.
Wie ist Deine Familie?
Schreib bald!
Udo

1 Die Postkarte ist von Udo. ________
2 Udo ist acht Jahre alt. ________
3 Udo hat zwei Geschwister. ________
4 Die Katze heißt Tobias. ________
5 Die Katze ist zehn Jahre alt. ________
6 Udos Geschwister haben zwei Kaninchen. ________

GLOSSARY
3C Which word is missing?
3D Read the postcard and the sentences. Which sentences are correct and which are wrong?

Zickzack neu 1 © Judy Somerville 1993 Published by Thomas Nelson & Sons Ltd 19

AT4 1

AT4 2
AT3 1

AT4 2
AT3 2

3 Meine Familie — Schreiben

3A *Welches Wort paßt zu welchem Bild? Beschrifte die Bilder.*

Beispiel 1 der Fisch

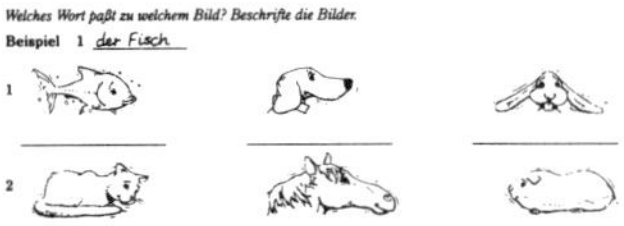

der Fisch	das Kaninchen	die Katze
das Meerschweinchen	das Pferd	der Hund

3B *Schreib die Wörter in der richtigen Reihenfolge auf.*

Beispiel 1 Hast du Geschwister?

1 Geschwister du Hast? ________
2 zwei habe Schwestern Ich. ________
3 Bruder heißt Paul Mein. ________
4 habe keine Ich Haustiere. ________
5 alt deine ist Wie Schwester? ________
6 eine zwei habe Brüder Schwester und Ich ________

3C *Schreib diese Sätze noch einmal mit Wörtern statt Bilder.*

Beispiel 1 Ich habe einen Hund.

1 ________
2 ________
3 ________

GLOSSARY
3A Which word goes with which picture? Label the pictures.
3B Write the words in the correct order.
3C Write these sentences again, with words instead of pictures.

20 Zickzack neu 1 © Judy Somerville 1993 Published by Thomas Nelson & Sons Ltd

KAPITEL 4

AT1 1

AT1 1

4 Bei mir zu Hause — Hören

4A *Hör gut zu und füll die Hausnummern aus.*

Beispiel Dieter: Hauptstraße 78

Name	Straße	Hausnummer
Dieter	Hauptstraße	
Sara	Rheinstraße	
Nils	Zum Sandweg	
Nina	Sommergasse	
Josef	Bergmannstraße	
Heidi	Am Marktplatz	

4B *Welche Telefonnummer gehört welcher Person?*

Beispiel 1 Erich B

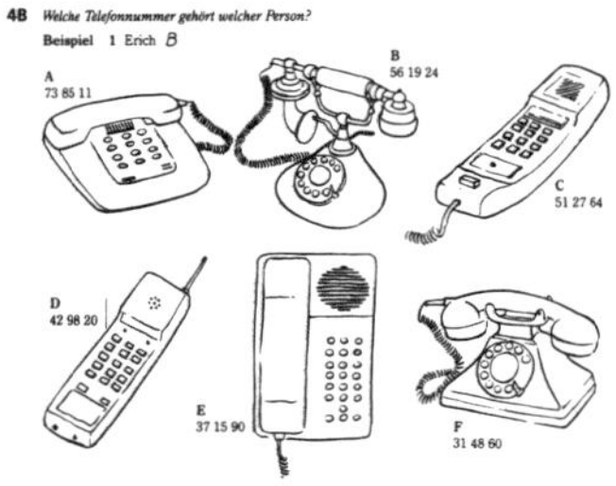

1 Erich ___
2 Kerstin ___
3 Ingrid ___
4 Peter ___
5 Fatima ___
6 Martin ___

GLOSSARY
4A Listen carefully and fill in the house numbers.
4B Which telephone number belongs to which person?

Zickzack neu 1 © Judy Somerville 1993 Published by Thomas Nelson & Sons Ltd 21

AT1 2

AT1 2,3
AT3 1

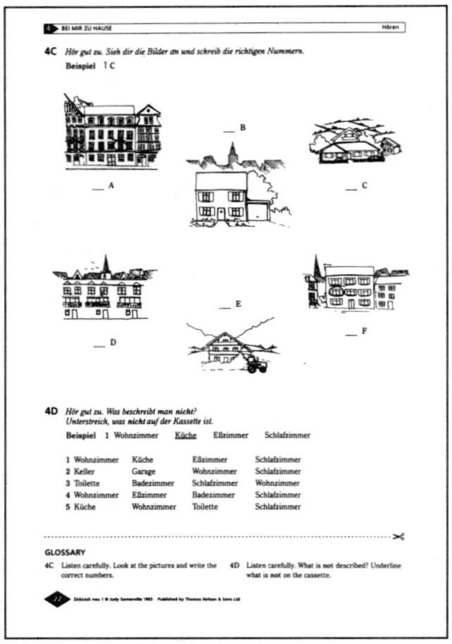

BEI MIR ZU HAUSE — Hören

4C *Hör gut zu. Sieh dir die Bilder an und schreib die richtigen Nummern.*

Beispiel 1 C

__ A __ B __ C __ D __ E __ F

4D *Hör gut zu. Was beschreibt man nicht? Unterstreich, was nicht auf der Kassette ist.*

Beispiel 1 Wohnzimmer Küche Eßzimmer Schlafzimmer

1 Wohnzimmer	Küche	Eßzimmer	Schlafzimmer
2 Keller	Garage	Wohnzimmer	Schlafzimmer
3 Toilette	Badezimmer	Schlafzimmer	Wohnzimmer
4 Wohnzimmer	Eßzimmer	Badezimmer	Schlafzimmer
5 Küche	Wohnzimmer	Toilette	Schlafzimmer

GLOSSARY

4C Listen carefully. Look at the pictures and write the correct numbers.

4D Listen carefully. What is not described? Underline what is not on the cassette.

22 Zickzack neu 1 © Judy Somerville 1993 Published by Thomas Nelson & Sons Ltd

AT2 1

AT2 2

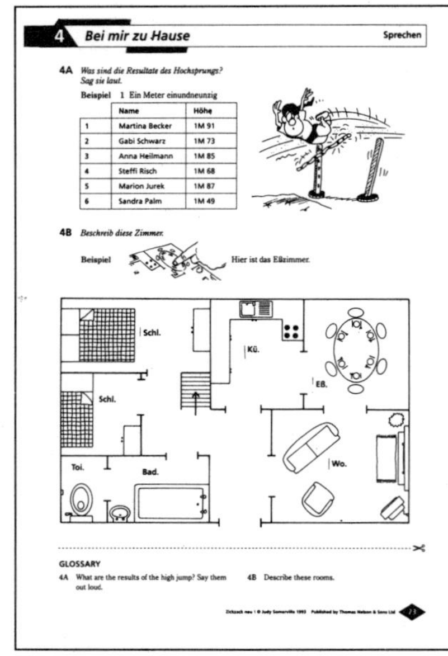

4 Bei mir zu Hause — Sprechen

4A *Was sind die Resultate des Hochsprungs? Sag sie laut.*

Beispiel 1 Ein Meter einundneunzig

	Name	Höhe
1	Martina Becker	1M 91
2	Gabi Schwarz	1M 73
3	Anna Heilmann	1M 85
4	Steffi Risch	1M 68
5	Marion Jurek	1M 87
6	Sandra Palm	1M 49

4B *Beschreib diese Zimmer.*

Beispiel Hier ist das Eßzimmer.

GLOSSARY

4A What are the results of the high jump? Say them out loud.

4B Describe these rooms.

Zickzack neu 1 © Judy Somerville 1993 Published by Thomas Nelson & Sons Ltd 23

AT2 2,3
AT1 2
AT3 2

AT2 2

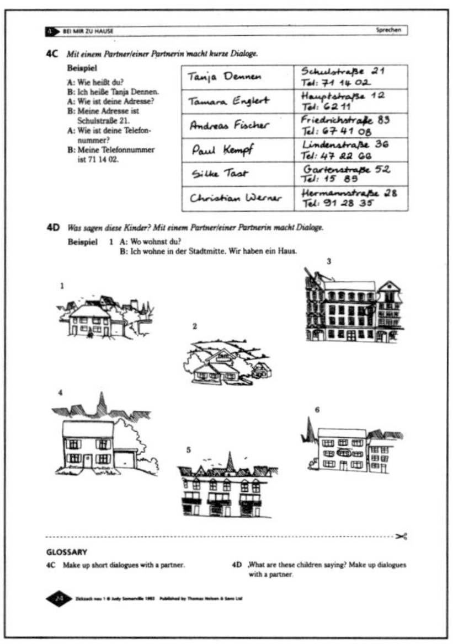

BEI MIR ZU HAUSE — Sprechen

4C *Mit einem Partner/einer Partnerin macht kurze Dialoge.*

Beispiel

A: Wie heißt du?
B: Ich heiße Tanja Dennen.
A: Wie ist deine Adresse?
B: Meine Adresse ist Schulstraße 21.
A: Wie ist deine Telefonnummer?
B: Meine Telefonnummer ist 71 14 02.

Tanja Dennen	Schulstraße 21 Tel: 71 14 02
Tamara Englert	Hauptstraße 12 Tel: 62 11
Andreas Fischer	Friedrichstraße 83 Tel: 67 41 08
Paul Kempf	Lindenstraße 36 Tel: 47 22 66
Silke Tast	Gartenstraße 52 Tel: 15 89
Christian Werner	Hermannstraße 28 Tel: 91 28 35

4D *Was sagen diese Kinder? Mit einem Partner/einer Partnerin macht Dialoge.*

Beispiel 1 A: Wo wohnst du?
B: Ich wohne in der Stadtmitte. Wir haben ein Haus.

1 2 3 4 5 6

GLOSSARY

4C Make up short dialogues with a partner.

4D What are these children saying? Make up dialogues with a partner.

24 Zickzack neu 1 © Judy Somerville 1993 Published by Thomas Nelson & Sons Ltd

AT3 1

AT3 2

AT3 2,3

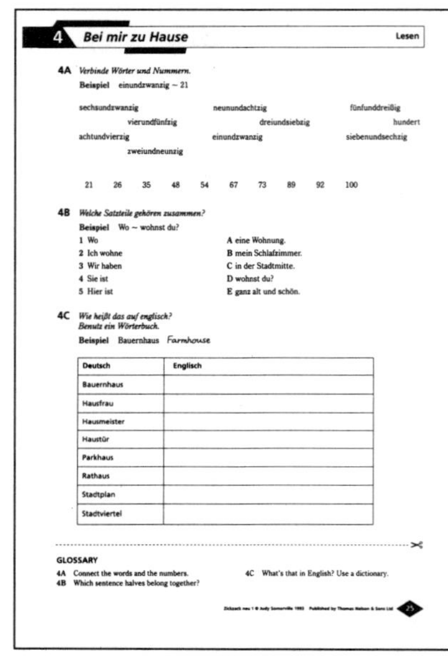

4 Bei mir zu Hause — Lesen

4A *Verbinde Wörter und Nummern.*

Beispiel einundzwanzig ~ 21

sechsundzwanzig, neunundachtzig, fünfunddreißig, vierundfünfzig, dreiundsiebzig, hundert, achtundvierzig, einundzwanzig, siebenundsechzig, zweiundneunzig

21 26 35 48 54 67 73 89 92 100

4B *Welche Satzteile gehören zusammen?*

Beispiel Wo ~ wohnst du?

1 Wo — A eine Wohnung.
2 Ich wohne — B mein Schlafzimmer.
3 Wir haben — C in der Stadtmitte.
4 Sie ist — D wohnst du?
5 Hier ist — E ganz alt und schön.

4C *Wie heißt das auf englisch? Benutz ein Wörterbuch.*

Beispiel Bauernhaus Farmhouse

Deutsch	Englisch
Bauernhaus	
Hausfrau	
Hausmeister	
Haustür	
Parkhaus	
Rathaus	
Stadtplan	
Stadtviertel	

GLOSSARY

4A Connect the words and the numbers.
4B Which sentence halves belong together?
4C What's that in English? Use a dictionary.

Zickzack neu 1 © Judy Somerville 1993 Published by Thomas Nelson & Sons Ltd 25

AT3 3

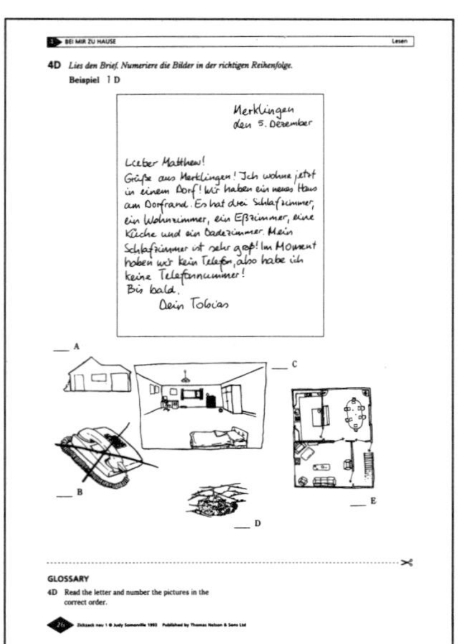

BEI MIR ZU HAUSE — Lesen

4D *Lies den Brief. Numeriere die Bilder in der richtigen Reihenfolge.*

Beispiel 1 D

Merklingen
den 5. Dezember

Lieber Matthew!
Grüße aus Merklingen! Ich wohne jetzt in einem Dorf! Wir haben ein neues Haus am Dorfrand. Es hat drei Schlafzimmer, ein Wohnzimmer, ein Eßzimmer, eine Küche und ein Badezimmer. Mein Schlafzimmer ist sehr groß! Im Moment haben wir kein Telefon, also habe ich keine Telefonnummer!
Bis bald.
Dein Tobias

__ A __ B __ C __ D __ E

GLOSSARY

4D Read the letter and number the pictures in the correct order.

26 Zickzack neu 1 © Judy Somerville 1993 Published by Thomas Nelson & Sons Ltd

AT4 1
AT3 2

AT4 2
AT3 2

AT4 2

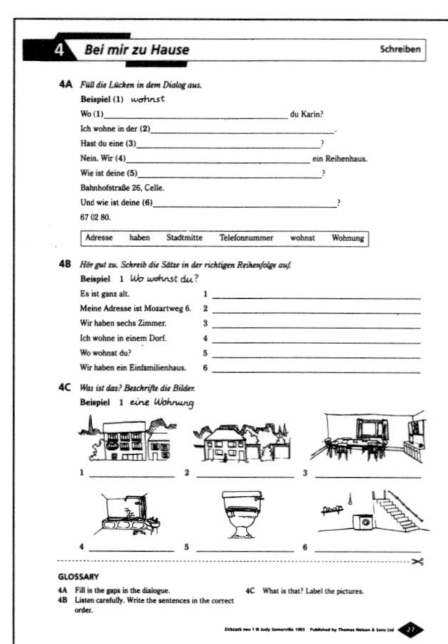

4 Bei mir zu Hause — Schreiben

4A *Füll die Lücken in dem Dialog aus.*

Beispiel (1) wohnst

Wo (1)________ du Karin?
Ich wohne in der (2)________.
Hast du eine (3)________?
Nein. Wir (4)________ ein Reihenhaus.
Wie ist deine (5)________?
Bahnhofstraße 26, Celle.
Und wie ist deine (6)________?
67 02 80.

Adresse haben Stadtmitte Telefonnummer wohnst Wohnung

4B *Hör gut zu. Schreib die Sätze in der richtigen Reihenfolge auf.*

Beispiel 1 Wo wohnst du?

Es ist ganz alt. 1 ________
Meine Adresse ist Mozartweg 6. 2 ________
Wir haben sechs Zimmer. 3 ________
Ich wohne in einem Dorf. 4 ________
Wo wohnst du? 5 ________
Wir haben ein Einfamilienhaus. 6 ________

4C *Was ist das? Beschrifte die Bilder.*

Beispiel 1 eine Wohnung

1 ____ 2 ____ 3 ____
4 ____ 5 ____ 6 ____

GLOSSARY

4A Fill in the gaps in the dialogue.
4B Listen carefully. Write the sentences in the correct order.
4C What is that? Label the pictures.

Zickzack neu 1 © Judy Somerville 1993 Published by Thomas Nelson & Sons Ltd 27

KAPITEL 5

AT1 1

5 Mein Alltag — Hören

5A *Hör gut zu. Füll die Uhren aus.*

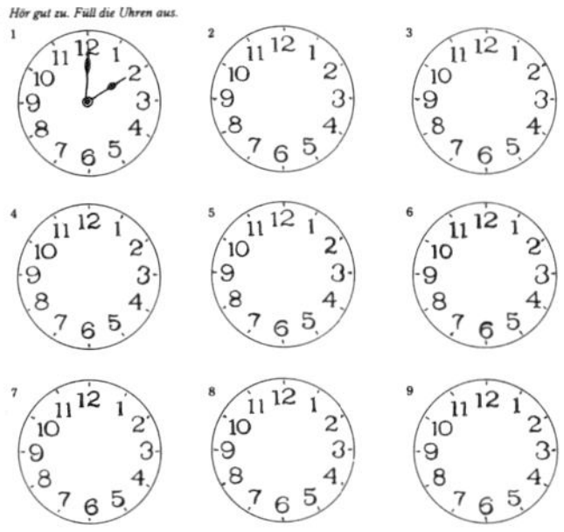

AT1 1

5B *Hör gut zu. Verbinde die Kinder mit ihren Geburtstagen.*

Beispiel Jens – 14.4.

Jens Jutta Markus Alexander Petra Oliver Brigitte Nadine

GLOSSARY

5A Listen carefully. Fill in the clocks.

5B Listen carefully. Join the children to their birthdays.

AT1 2

5C *Hör gut zu. Füll die Video-Informationen aus.*

Beispiel
Formel eins 27.5. 12:45

Sendung	Datum	Zeit
Formel eins		
Guten Morgen		
Horoskop		
Yogi Bär		
Raumschiff Enterprise		
Sport extra		

AT1 2
AT3 2

5D *Wer macht was? Hör gut zu. Mach jedesmal einen Haken in die richtige Spalte.*

	ich gehe in die Stadt	ich mache meine Hausaufgaben	ich treffe mich mit Freunden	ich esse	ich sehe fern	ich gehe ins Bett
Anna					✔	✔
Ralf						
Kasimir						
Sabine						
Dorit						
Werner						

GLOSSARY

5C Listen carefully. Fill in the video information.

5D Who does what? Listen carefully. Put ticks in the right columns each time.

5 Mein Alltag — Sprechen

AT2 1

5A *Wie spät ist es? Sag die Uhrzeit.*

Beispiel 1 Es ist sieben Uhr.

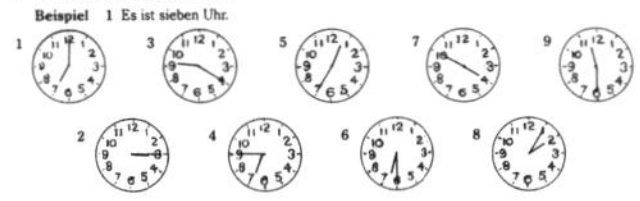

AT2 2

5B *Du bist Popstar! Sieh dir die Bilder an und beschreib deinen Alltag.*

Beispiel Es ist Viertel vor zwei. Ich stehe auf.

AT2 2

5C *Arbeitet zu zweit.*
Person A stellt die Frage „Wann hast du Geburtstag?"
Person B antwortet mit einem Datum rechts.

Beispiel 1 Ich habe am vierzehnten März Geburtstag.

Dann stellt Person B die Frage.

AT2 3

5D *Beschreib jetzt deinen Alltag in zirka sechs Sätzen.*

Beispiel Ich stehe (um Viertel vor sieben) auf.
Ich wasche mich (um zehn vor sieben).

GLOSSARY

5A What time is it? Say the time.

5B You are a pop star. Look at the pictures and describe your daily routine.

5C Work in pairs. Person A asks the question "When's your birthday?" Person B answers with a date from the right. Then Person B asks the question.

5D Now describe your daily routine in about six sentences.

5 Mein Alltag — Lesen

AT3 1

5A *Welche Uhr paßt zu welcher Zeit?*

Beispiel 1 F

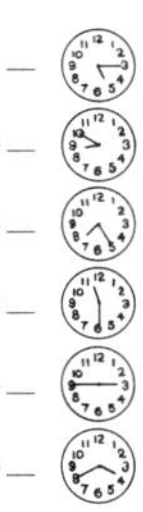

1 ___ A Viertel vor drei

2 ___ B fünfundzwanzig nach sieben

3 ___ C zehn vor neun

4 ___ D zwanzig vor vier

5 ___ E halb zwölf

6 ___ F Viertel nach fünf

AT3 2

5B *Welches Wort fehlt?*

Beispiel 1 D

1 Ich habe am 3. Mai ____. A treffe

2 Ich ____ um sieben Uhr auf. B verlasse

3 Ich ____ das Haus um halb acht. C beginnt

4 Der Unterricht ____ um acht Uhr. D Geburtstag

5 Nachmittags mache ich meine ____. E Hausaufgaben

6 Dann ____ ich mich mit Freunden. F stehe

GLOSSARY

5A Which clock matches which time?

5B Which word is missing?

AT3 2

5C *Verbinde die Sätze und die Bilder.*

Beispiel 1 – Ich sehe fern.

Ich gehe ins Bett.

Ich frühstücke.

Ich sehe fern.

Ich treffe mich mit Freunden.

Die Schule ist aus.

Ich wasche mich.

AT3 3
AT4 1

5D *Lies diesen Brief.*

Jena,
den 8. Oktober

Lieber Jörg,
wie geht's? Was machst Du? Ich habe am 14. Oktober Geburtstag. Am Morgen treffe ich mich mit Freunden, und ich gehe in die Stadt. Dann komme ich wieder nach Hause und esse, und am Nachmittag gebe ich eine Party!
Kommst Du mit?
Viele Grüße,
Michael

Sind diese Sätze richtig oder falsch?

Beispiel
1 falsch

1 Der Brief ist von Jörg. ________

2 Michael ist 14 Jahre alt. ________

3 Er hat im Oktober Geburtstag. ________

4 Er geht in die Schule. ________

5 Die Party ist am Nachmittag. ________

GLOSSARY

5C Join the sentences and the pictures.

5D Read the letter. Are these sentences true or false?

5 Mein Alltag — Schreiben

AT4 1

5A *Welcher Monat ist das?*

Beispiel 1 Oktober

Januar	März	Oktober
Februar	Juni	Dezember

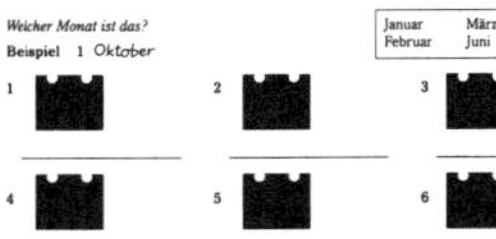

AT4 2
AT3 2

5B *Schreib den Dialog in der richtigen Reihenfolge auf. (Viele Dialoge sind möglich!)*

Wann hast du Geburtstag? ________________

Ich treffe mich mit Freunden. ________________

Wie alt bist du? ________________

Ich habe am 21. Juli Geburtstag. ________________

Was machst du? ________________

Ich bin dreizehn Jahre alt. ________________

AT4 2
AT3 2

5C *Füll das Kreuzworträtsel aus.*

Waagerecht (→)

4 Ich ______ mich um 7:00.

6 Ich ______ mich mit Freunden.

7 Was ______ du an deinem Geburtstag?

9 Wann hast du ______ ?

12 Ich ______ im Restaurant.

13 9:05 = fünf nach ______.

14 Ich sehe ______.

Senkrecht (↓)

1 Ich mache meine ——.

2 4:00 = vier ——.

3 10:15 = —— nach zehn.

5 Der Unterricht —— um 9:00.

8 Die —— ist aus.

10 Ich —— um 6:45 auf.

11 Ich —— in die Stadt.

GLOSSARY

5A Which month is that?

5B Write the dialogue in the correct order. (Lots of dialogues are possible!)

5C Fill in the crossword.

KAPITEL 6

AT1 1

AT1 2,3
AT3 1

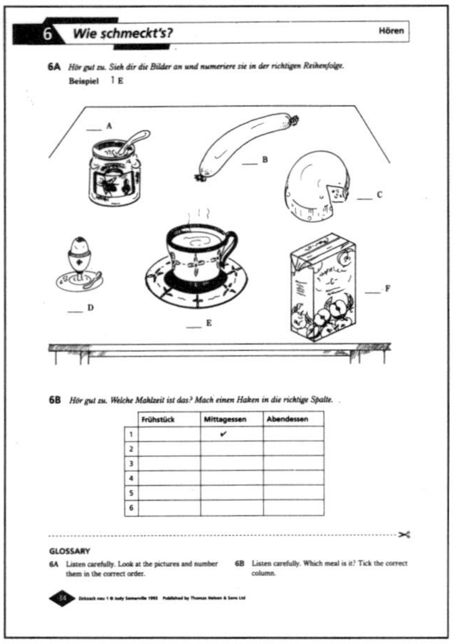

6 **Wie schmeckt's?** Hören

6A *Hör gut zu. Sieh dir die Bilder an und numeriere sie in der richtigen Reihenfolge.*

Beispiel 1 E

6B *Hör gut zu. Welche Mahlzeit ist das? Mach einen Haken in die richtige Spalte.*

	Frühstück	Mittagessen	Abendessen
1		✔	
2			
3			
4			
5			
6			

GLOSSARY

6A Listen carefully. Look at the pictures and number them in the correct order.

6B Listen carefully. Which meal is it? Tick the correct column.

34 Zickzack neu 1 © Judy Somerville 1993 Published by Thomas Nelson & Sons Ltd

AT1 3
AT3 1

AT1 3

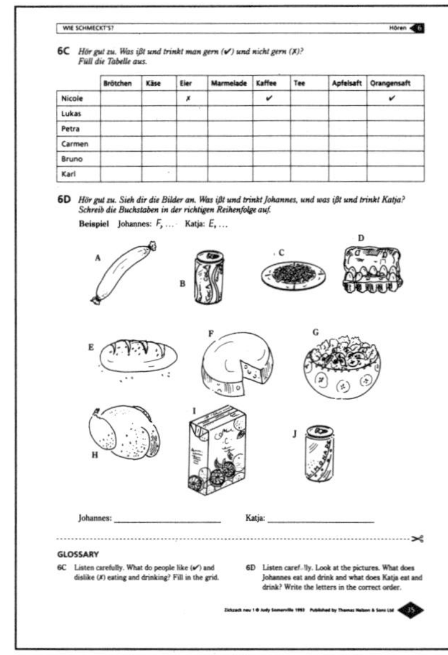

WIE SCHMECKT'S? Hören 6

6C *Hör gut zu. Was ißt und trinkt man gern (✔) und nicht gern (✗)? Füll die Tabelle aus.*

	Brötchen	Käse	Eier	Marmelade	Kaffee	Tee	Apfelsaft	Orangensaft
Nicole			✗		✔			✔
Lukas								
Petra								
Carmen								
Bruno								
Karl								

6D *Hör gut zu. Sieh dir die Bilder an. Was ißt und trinkt Johannes, und was ißt und trinkt Katja? Schreib die Buchstaben in der richtigen Reihenfolge auf.*

Beispiel Johannes: F, … Katja: E, …

Johannes: ______________ Katja: ______________

GLOSSARY

6C Listen carefully. What do people like (✔) and dislike (✗) eating and drinking? Fill in the grid.

6D Listen caref.·lly. Look at the pictures. What does Johannes eat and drink and what does Katja eat and drink? Write the letters in the correct order.

Zickzack neu 1 © Judy Somerville 1993 Published by Thomas Nelson & Sons Ltd 35

AT2 1

AT2 2

6 **Wie schmeckt's?** Sprechen

6A *Was ist das?*

Beispiel 1 Orangensaft

6B *Mit einem Partner/einer Partnerin macht Dialoge.*

Beispiel 1 A: Was ißt und trinkst du zum Frühstück?
B: Ich esse Brötchen und Marmelade, und ich trinke Kaffee und Apfelsaft.

GLOSSARY

6A What is that?

6B Make up dialogues with a partner.

36 Zickzack neu 1 © Judy Somerville 1993 Published by Thomas Nelson & Sons Ltd

AT2 3
AT1 2

AT2 3

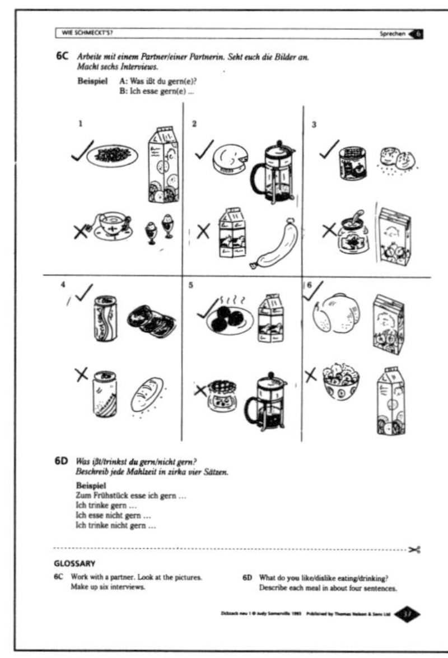

WIE SCHMECKT'S? Sprechen 6

6C *Arbeite mit einem Partner/einer Partnerin. Seht euch die Bilder an. Macht sechs Interviews.*

Beispiel A: Was ißt du gern(e)?
B: Ich esse gern(e) …

6D *Was ißt/trinkst du gern/nicht gern? Beschreib jede Mahlzeit in zirka vier Sätzen.*

Beispiel
Zum Frühstück esse ich gern …
Ich trinke gern …
Ich esse nicht gern …
Ich trinke nicht gern …

GLOSSARY

6C Work with a partner. Look at the pictures. Make up six interviews.

6D What do you like/dislike eating/drinking? Describe each meal in about four sentences.

Zickzack neu 1 © Judy Somerville 1993 Published by Thomas Nelson & Sons Ltd 37

AT3 1

AT3 2

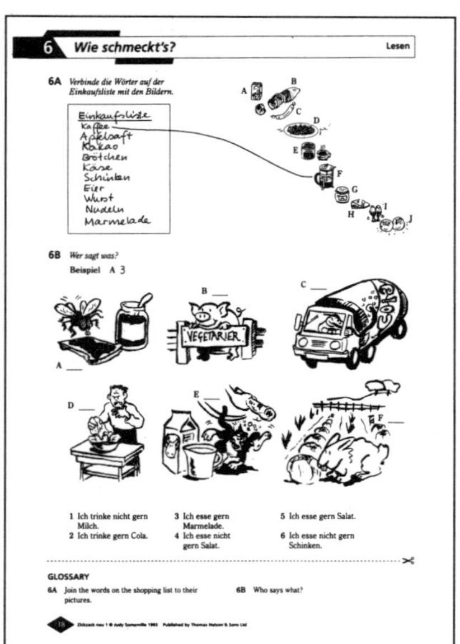

6 **Wie schmeckt's?** Lesen

6A *Verbinde die Wörter auf der Einkaufsliste mit den Bildern.*

6B *Wer sagt was?*

Beispiel A 3

1 Ich trinke nicht gern Milch.
2 Ich trinke gern Cola.
3 Ich esse gern Marmelade.
4 Ich esse nicht gern Salat.
5 Ich esse gern Salat.
6 Ich esse nicht gern Schinken.

GLOSSARY

6A Join the words on the shopping list to their pictures.

6B Who says what?

38 Zickzack neu 1 © Judy Somerville 1993 Published by Thomas Nelson & Sons Ltd

AT3 2

AT3 3

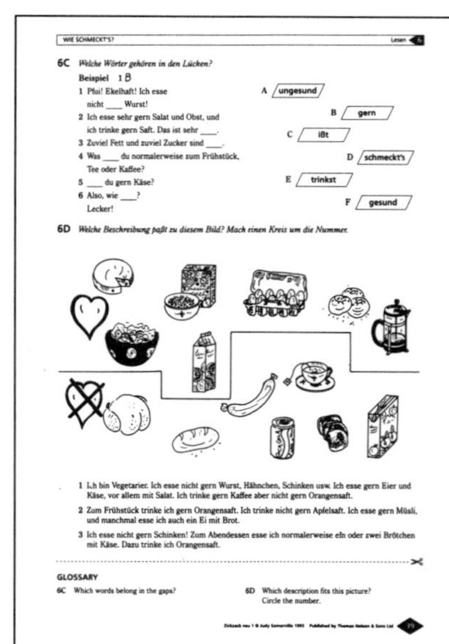

WIE SCHMECKT'S? Lesen 6

6C *Welche Wörter gehören in den Lücken?*

Beispiel 1 B

1 Pfui! Ekelhaft! Ich esse nicht ____ Wurst!
2 Ich esse sehr gern Salat und Obst, und ich trinke gern Saft. Das ist sehr ____.
3 Zuviel Fett und zuviel Zucker sind ____.
4 Was ____ du normalerweise zum Frühstück, Tee oder Kaffee?
5 ____ du gern Käse?
6 Also, wie ____?
Lecker!

A ungesund
B gern
C ißt
D schmeckt's
E trinkst
F gesund

6D *Welche Beschreibung paßt zu diesem Bild? Mach einen Kreis um die Nummer.*

1 Ich bin Vegetarier. Ich esse nicht gern Wurst, Hähnchen, Schinken usw. Ich esse gern Eier und Käse, vor allem mit Salat. Ich trinke gern Kaffee aber nicht gern Orangensaft.
2 Zum Frühstück trinke ich gern Orangensaft. Ich trinke nicht gern Apfelsaft. Ich esse gern Müsli, und manchmal esse ich auch ein Ei mit Brot.
3 Ich esse nicht gern Schinken! Zum Abendessen esse ich normalerweise ein oder zwei Brötchen mit Käse. Dazu trinke ich Orangensaft.

GLOSSARY

6C Which words belong in the gaps?

6D Which description fits this picture? Circle the number.

Zickzack neu 1 © Judy Somerville 1993 Published by Thomas Nelson & Sons Ltd 39

AT4 1

AT4 2
AT3 1

AT4 3
AT3 2

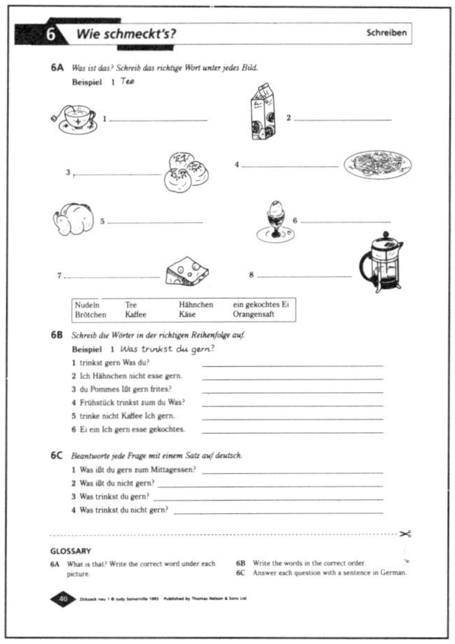
6 **Wie schmeckt's?** Schreiben

6A *Was ist das? Schreib das richtige Wort unter jedes Bild.*
Beispiel 1 Tee

Nudeln	Tee	Hähnchen	ein gekochtes Ei
Brötchen	Kaffee	Käse	Orangensaft

6B *Schreib die Wörter in der richtigen Reihenfolge auf.*
Beispiel 1 Was trinkst du gern?
1 trinkst gern Was du?
2 Ich Hähnchen nicht esse gern.
3 du Pommes ißt gern frites?
4 Frühstück trinkst zum du Was?
5 trinke nicht Kaffee Ich gern.
6 Ei ein Ich gern esse gekochtes.

6C *Beantworte jede Frage mit einem Satz auf deutsch.*
1 Was ißt du gern zum Mittagessen?
2 Was ißt du nicht gern?
3 Was trinkst du gern?
4 Was trinkst du nicht gern?

GLOSSARY
6A What is that? Write the correct word under each picture.
6B Write the words in the correct order.
6C Answer each question with a sentence in German.

40

KAPITEL 7

AT1 1

AT1 2

AT1 3

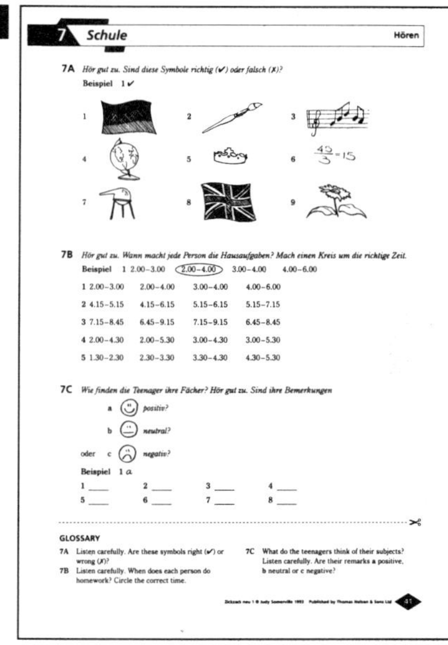
7 **Schule** Hören

7A *Hör gut zu. Sind diese Symbole richtig (✔) oder falsch (✘)?*
Beispiel 1 ✔

7B *Hör gut zu. Wann macht jede Person die Hausaufgaben? Mach einen Kreis um die richtige Zeit.*
Beispiel 1 2.00–3.00 (2.00–4.00) 3.00–4.00 4.00–6.00

1	2.00–3.00	2.00–4.00	3.00–4.00	4.00–6.00
2	4.15–5.15	4.15–6.15	5.15–6.15	5.15–7.15
3	7.15–8.45	6.45–9.15	7.15–9.15	6.45–8.45
4	2.00–4.30	2.00–5.30	3.00–4.30	3.00–5.30
5	1.30–2.30	2.30–3.30	3.30–4.30	4.30–5.30

7C *Wie finden die Teenager ihre Fächer? Hör gut zu. Sind ihre Bemerkungen*
a positiv?
b neutral?
oder c negativ?
Beispiel 1 a

GLOSSARY
7A Listen carefully. Are these symbols right (✔) or wrong (✘)?
7B Listen carefully. When does each person do homework? Circle the correct time.
7C What do the teenagers think of their subjects? Listen carefully. Are their remarks a positive, b neutral or c negative?

41

AT2 1

AT2 1
AT1 1
AT2 1,2
AT3 2
AT2 2,3,4
AT1 2

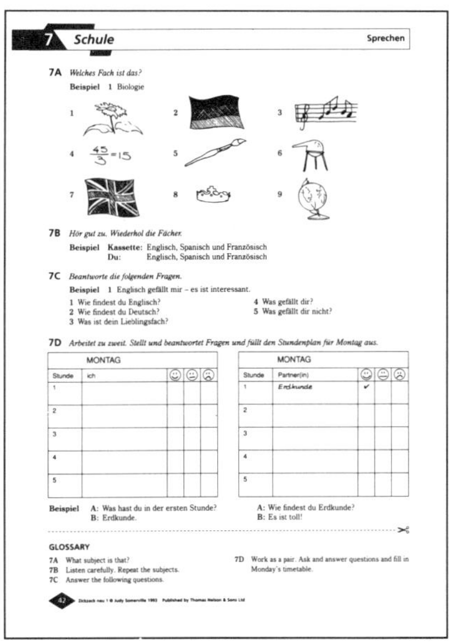
7 **Schule** Sprechen

7A *Welches Fach ist das?*
Beispiel 1 Biologie

7B *Hör gut zu. Wiederhol die Fächer.*
Beispiel Kassette: Englisch, Spanisch und Französisch
Du: Englisch, Spanisch und Französisch

7C *Beantworte die folgenden Fragen.*
Beispiel 1 Englisch gefällt mir – es ist interessant.
1 Wie findest du Englisch?
2 Wie findest du Deutsch?
3 Was ist dein Lieblingsfach?
4 Was gefällt dir?
5 Was gefällt dir nicht?

7D *Arbeitet zu zweit. Stellt und beantwortet Fragen und füllt den Stundenplan für Montag aus.*

MONTAG

Stunde	Ich			
1				
2				
3				
4				
5				

MONTAG

Stunde	Partner(in)			
1	Erdkunde	✔		
2				
3				
4				
5				

Beispiel A: Was hast du in der ersten Stunde?
B: Erdkunde.
A: Wie findest du Erdkunde?
B: Es ist toll!

GLOSSARY
7A What subject is that?
7B Listen carefully. Repeat the subjects.
7C Answer the following questions.
7D Work as a pair. Ask and answer questions and fill in Monday's timetable.

42

AT3 1

AT3 2,3

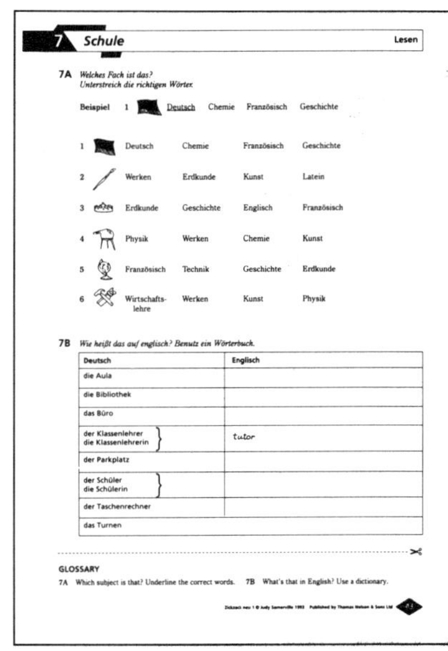
7 **Schule** Lesen

7A *Welches Fach ist das? Unterstreich die richtigen Wörter.*
Beispiel 1 Deutsch Chemie Französisch Geschichte

1	Deutsch	Chemie	Französisch	Geschichte
2	Werken	Erdkunde	Kunst	Latein
3	Erdkunde	Geschichte	Englisch	Französisch
4	Physik	Werken	Chemie	Kunst
5	Französisch	Technik	Geschichte	Erdkunde
6	Wirtschaftslehre	Werken	Kunst	Physik

7B *Wie heißt das auf englisch? Benutz ein Wörterbuch.*

Deutsch	Englisch
die Aula	
die Bibliothek	
das Büro	
der Klassenlehrer / die Klassenlehrerin	tutor
der Parkplatz	
der Schüler / die Schülerin	
der Taschenrechner	
das Turnen	

GLOSSARY
7A Which subject is that? Underline the correct words.
7B What's that in English? Use a dictionary.

43

AT3 4

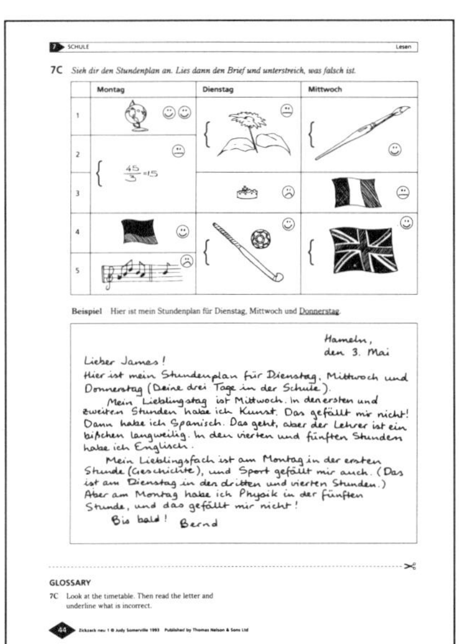
7 SCHULE Lesen

7C *Sieh dir den Stundenplan an. Lies dann den Brief und unterstreich, was falsch ist.*

	Montag	Dienstag	Mittwoch
1			
2			
3			
4			
5			

Beispiel Hier ist mein Stundenplan für Dienstag, Mittwoch und Donnerstag.

Hameln, den 3. Mai

Lieber James!
Hier ist mein Stundenplan für Dienstag, Mittwoch und Donnerstag (Deine drei Tage in der Schule).
Mein Lieblingstag ist Mittwoch. In den ersten und zweiten Stunden habe ich Kunst. Das gefällt mir nicht! Dann habe ich Spanisch. Das geht, aber der Lehrer ist ein bißchen langweilig. In den vierten und fünften Stunden habe ich Englisch.
Mein Lieblingsfach ist am Montag in der ersten Stunde (Geschichte), und Sport gefällt mir auch. (Das ist am Dienstag in der dritten und vierten Stunden.) Aber am Montag habe ich Physik in der fünften Stunde, und das gefällt mir nicht!
Bis bald! Bernd

GLOSSARY
7C Look at the timetable. Then read the letter and underline what is incorrect.

44

AT4 1

AT4 2
AT3 2

AT4 3,4

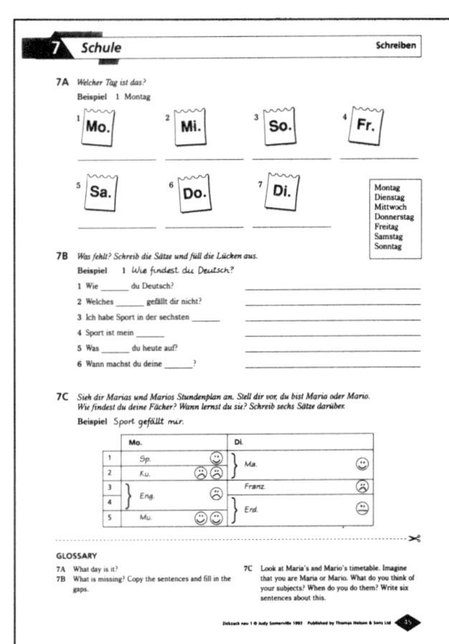
7 **Schule** Schreiben

7A *Welcher Tag ist das?*
Beispiel 1 Montag
1 Mo. 2 Mi. 3 So. 4 Fr. 5 Sa. 6 Do. 7 Di.

Montag
Dienstag
Mittwoch
Donnerstag
Freitag
Samstag
Sonntag

7B *Was fehlt? Schreib die Sätze und füll die Lücken aus.*
Beispiel 1 Wie findest du Deutsch?
1 Wie ______ du Deutsch?
2 Welches ______ gefällt dir nicht?
3 Ich habe Sport in der sechsten ______
4 Sport ist mein ______
5 Was ______ du heute auf?
6 Wann machst du deine ______?

7C *Sieh dir Marias und Marios Stundenplan an. Stell dir vor, du bist Maria oder Mario. Wie findest du deine Fächer? Wann lernst du sie? Schreib sechs Sätze darüber.*
Beispiel Sport gefällt mir.

	Mo.	Di.
1	Sp.	Ma.
2	Ku.	
3	Eng.	Franz.
4		Erd.
5	Mu.	

GLOSSARY
7A What day is it?
7B What is missing? Copy the sentences and fill in the gaps.
7C Look at Maria's and Mario's timetable. Imagine that you are Maria or Mario. What do you think of your subjects? When do you do them? Write six sentences about this.

45

KAPITEL 8

AT1 1

AT1 1

AT1 2

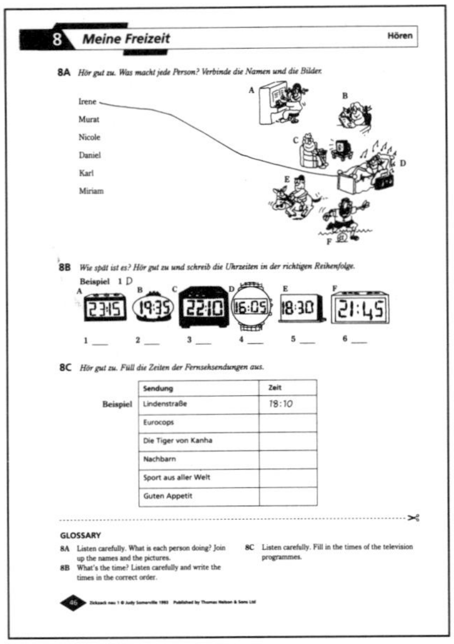
8 Meine Freizeit — Hören

8A *Hör gut zu. Was macht jede Person? Verbinde die Namen und die Bilder.*

Irene
Murat
Nicole
Daniel
Karl
Miriam

8B *Wie spät ist es? Hör gut zu und schreib die Uhrzeiten in der richtigen Reihenfolge.*

Beispiel 1 D

A 23:15 B 19:35 C 22:10 D 16:05 E 18:30 F 21:45

1 ___ 2 ___ 3 ___ 4 ___ 5 ___ 6 ___

8C *Hör gut zu. Füll die Zeiten der Fernsehsendungen aus.*

	Sendung	Zeit
Beispiel	Lindenstraße	18:10
	Eurocops	
	Die Tiger von Kanha	
	Nachbarn	
	Sport aus aller Welt	
	Guten Appetit	

GLOSSARY
8A Listen carefully. What is each person doing? Join up the names and the pictures.
8B What's the time? Listen carefully and write the times in the correct order.
8C Listen carefully. Fill in the times of the television programmes.

AT1 3

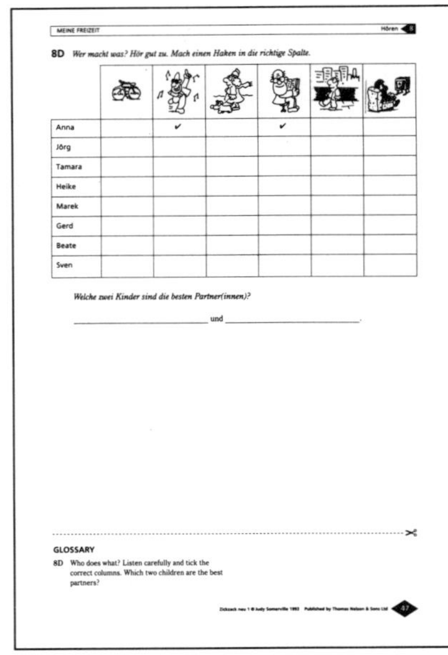
MEINE FREIZEIT — Hören 8

8D *Wer macht was? Hör gut zu. Mach einen Haken in die richtige Spalte.*

Anna		✓		✓		
Jörg						
Tamara						
Heike						
Marek						
Gerd						
Beate						
Sven						

Welche zwei Kinder sind die besten Partner(innen)?

_______________ und _______________.

GLOSSARY
8D Who does what? Listen carefully and tick the correct columns. Which two children are the best partners?

AT2 1
AT2 2,3
AT1 2

AT2 3,4
AT3 2

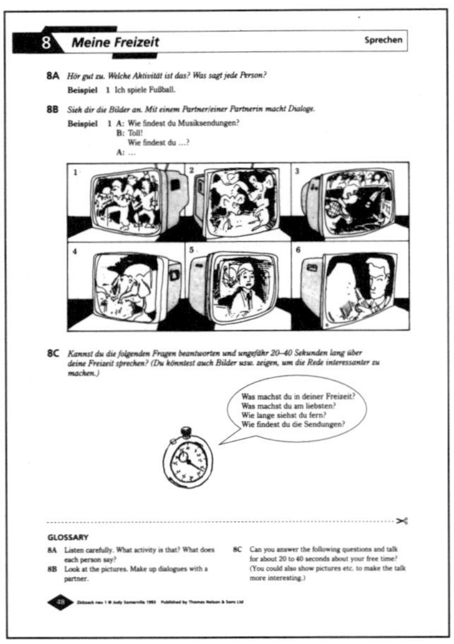
8 Meine Freizeit — Sprechen

8A *Hör gut zu. Welche Aktivität ist das? Was sagt jede Person?*
Beispiel 1 Ich spiele Fußball.

8B *Sieh dir die Bilder an. Mit einem Partner/einer Partnerin macht Dialoge.*
Beispiel 1 A: Wie findest du Musiksendungen?
B: Toll!
Wie findest du ...?
A: ...

8C *Kannst du die folgenden Fragen beantworten und ungefähr 20–40 Sekunden lang über deine Freizeit sprechen? (Du könntest auch Bilder usw. zeigen, um die Rede interessanter zu machen.)*

Was machst du in deiner Freizeit?
Was machst du am liebsten?
Wie lange siehst du fern?
Wie findest du die Sendungen?

GLOSSARY
8A Listen carefully. What activity is that? What does each person say?
8B Look at the pictures. Make up dialogues with a partner.
8C Can you answer the following questions and talk for about 20 to 40 seconds about your free time? (You could also show pictures etc. to make the talk more interesting.)

AT3 1

AT3 2

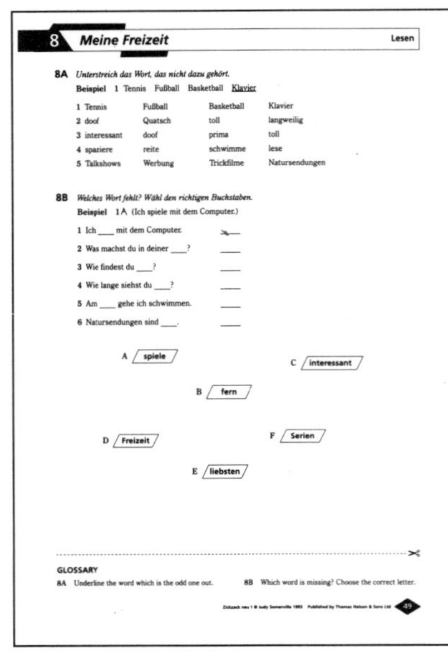
8 Meine Freizeit — Lesen

8A *Unterstreich das Wort, das nicht dazu gehört.*
Beispiel 1 Tennis Fußball Basketball Klavier

1 Tennis	Fußball	Basketball	Klavier
2 doof	Quatsch	toll	langweilig
3 interessant	doof	prima	toll
4 spaziere	reite	schwimme	lese
5 Talkshows	Werbung	Trickfilme	Natursendungen

8B *Welches Wort fehlt? Wähl den richtigen Buchstaben.*
Beispiel 1 A (Ich spiele mit dem Computer.)

1 Ich ___ mit dem Computer.
2 Was machst du in deiner ___?
3 Wie findest du ___?
4 Wie lange siehst du ___?
5 Am ___ gehe ich schwimmen.
6 Natursendungen sind ___.

A spiele
B fern
C interessant
D Freizeit
E liebsten
F Serien

GLOSSARY
8A Underline the word which is the odd one out.
8B Which word is missing? Choose the correct letter.

AT3 2

AT3 3

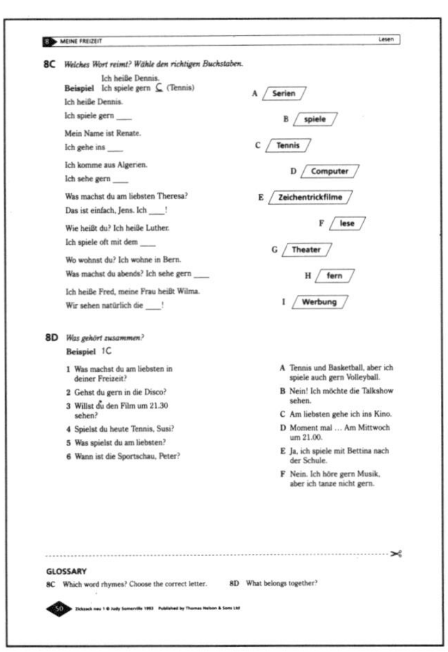
MEINE FREIZEIT — Lesen

8C *Welches Wort reimt? Wähle den richtigen Buchstaben.*

Beispiel Ich heiße Dennis. Ich spiele gern C (Tennis)

Ich heiße Dennis.
Ich spiele gern ___

Mein Name ist Renate.
Ich gehe ins ___

Ich komme aus Algerien.
Ich sehe gern ___

Was machst du am liebsten Theresa?
Das ist einfach, Jens. Ich ___!

Wie heißt du? Ich heiße Luther.
Ich spiele oft mit dem ___

Wo wohnst du? Ich wohne in Bern.
Was machst du abends? Ich sehe gern ___

Ich heiße Fred, meine Frau heißt Wilma.
Wir sehen natürlich die ___!

A Serien
B spiele
C Tennis
D Computer
E Zeichentrickfilme
F lese
G Theater
H fern
I Werbung

8D *Was gehört zusammen?*
Beispiel 1C

1 Was machst du am liebsten in deiner Freizeit?
2 Gehst du gern in die Disco?
3 Willst du den Film um 21.30 sehen?
4 Spielst du heute Tennis, Susi?
5 Was spielst du am liebsten?
6 Wann ist die Sportschau, Peter?

A Tennis und Basketball, aber ich spiele auch gern Volleyball.
B Nein! Ich möchte die Talkshow sehen.
C Am liebsten gehe ich ins Kino.
D Moment mal ... Am Mittwoch um 21.00.
E Ja, ich spiele mit Bettina nach der Schule.
F Nein. Ich höre gern Musik, aber ich tanze nicht gern.

GLOSSARY
8C Which word rhymes? Choose the correct letter.
8D What belongs together?

AT4 1

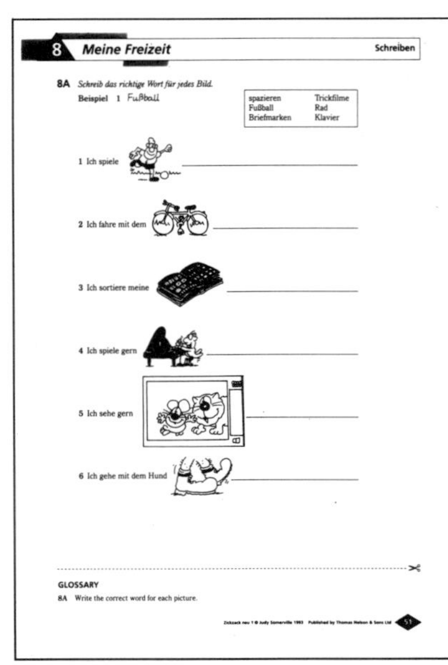
8 Meine Freizeit — Schreiben

8A *Schreib das richtige Wort für jedes Bild.*
Beispiel 1 Fußball

spazieren, Fußball, Briefmarken, Trickfilme, Rad, Klavier

1 Ich spiele ___
2 Ich fahre mit dem ___
3 Ich sortiere meine ___
4 Ich spiele gern ___
5 Ich sehe gern ___
6 Ich gehe mit dem Hund ___

GLOSSARY
8A Write the correct word for each picture.

AT4 2
AT3 2

8B *Füll das Rätsel aus. Wenn alle Antworten richtig sind, siehst du ein neuntes Wort!*

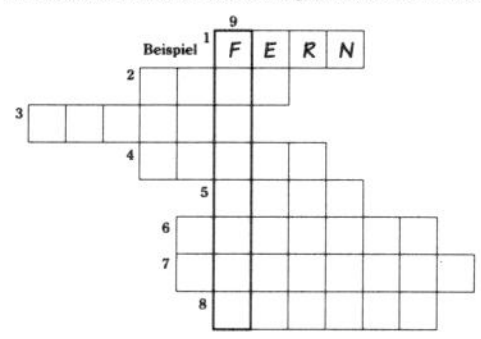

1 Ich sehe _______
2 Ich _______ gern Musik.
3 Ich _______ in der Stadt.
4 Ich habe ein Pferd und _______ gern.
5 Ich habe _______ Hunde, Max und Moritz.
6 „Tiere der Welt" ist eine _______
7 Was machst du am _______ in deiner Freizeit?
8 Ich _______ mich mit meinen Freunden.

AT4 3,4
AT3 3

8C *Du möchtest auch einen Brieffreund/eine Brieffreundin haben! Schreib eine Anzeige über deine Hobbys und Interessen.*

ICH SUCHE …

einen Brieffreund/eine Brieffreundin!
Ich heiße Claudia Elsner, und ich bin dreizehn Jahre alt. Ich spiele gern Tennis und höre gern Musik. Am liebsten fahre ich rad. Ich sehe gern fern – besonders Serien.

GLOSSARY

8B Fill in the puzzle. If all the answers are correct, you will see a ninth word!

8C You would also like a penfriend. Write an advert about your hobbies and interests.

KAPITEL 9

AT1 1

9 Was kostet das?

9A *Hör gut zu und füll die Preise aus.*

SPEISEKARTE	DM
Hamburger	4,9(
Bratwurst	
Frikadelle	
Pommes frites	
Eis	

AT1 2

9B *Sieh dir die Tabelle an und hör gut zu. Was stimmt nicht? Mach einen Kreis um das Imbiß, das Getränk oder den Preis.*

Beispiel 1 Bratwurst (Cola) 5,10 DM

	Imbiß	Getränk	Preis
1	Bratwurst	Cola	5,10 DM
2	2 X Pommes	Limonade	3, 90 DM
3	2 X Schaschlik	Apfelsaft	10,00 DM
4	Vanilleeis	2 X Cola	4,50 DM
5	Hamburger und Pommes	Apfelsaft	8,00 DM
6	2 X Erdbeereis	2 X Limonade	7,00 DM

AT1 3

9C *Hör gut zu. Sparen die Teenager ihr Geld oder geben sie es aus? Wofür? Sieh dir die Bilder an und schreib die Nummer in die richtige Spalte.*

GLOSSARY

9A Listen carefully and fill in the prices.

9B Look at the grid and listen carefully. What is not correct? Circle the snack, the drink or the price.

9C Listen carefully. Do the teenagers save their money or do they spend it? What do they save for or spend it on? Look at the pictures and write the numbers in the correct columns.

AT2 1

9 Was kostet das? Sprechen

9A *Was kostet das? Sag die Preise.*

Beispiel
1 Eine Mark und eine Mark neunundneunzig.
Das macht zwei Mark neunundneunzig.

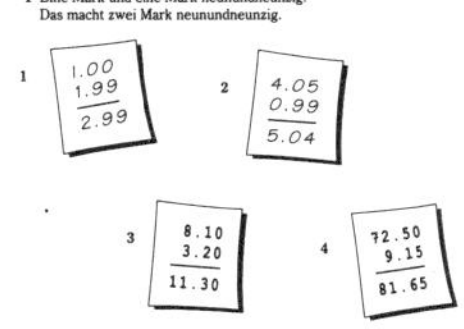

AT2 1,2
AT3 2

9B *Hör gut zu und wiederhol die Sätze.*

Beispiel
1 **Kassette:** Ich möchte ein Zitroneneis, bitte.
Du: Ich möchte ein Zitroneneis, bitte.

1 Ich möchte ein Zitroneneis, bitte.
2 Einmal Bratwurst und zwei Frikadellen, bitte.
3 Was macht das, bitte?
4 Ich spare für Turnschuhe.
5 Ich fahre mit Renates Riesenrad.

GLOSSARY

9A How much is that? Say the prices.

9B Listen carefully and repeat the sentences.

AT2 2
AT3 2

9C *Hier sind die Antworten. Was waren die Fragen?*

Beispiel 1 Was kostet das?

1 Das kostet eine Mark neunundneunzig.
2 Ich nehme eine Cola, bitte.
3 Ich spare mein Geld für ein Rad.
4 Ich gebe mein Geld für Kassetten aus.
5 Ja, aber am liebsten fahre ich mit der Geisterbahn.

AT2 3
AT1 2

9D *Sieh dir die Bilder an und mach Dialoge mit einem Partner/einer Partnerin.*

Beispiel
A: Was nimmst du, Martin?
B: Eine Cola und Pommes frites, bitte.
A: Und ich nehme eine Bratwurst, eine Portion Pommes und eine Cola. Also, eine Bratwurst, zwei Portionen Pommes und zweimal Cola, bitte.
B: Was nimmst du, Hella?

Name	mein Freund/ meine Freundin	ich
1 Martin		
2 Hella		
3 Friedrich		
4 Dagmar		
5 Hassan		
6 Tara		

GLOSSARY

9C Here are the answers. What were the questions?

9D Look at the pictures and make up dialogues with a partner.

AT3 1

9 Was kostet das? Lesen

9A *Für jedes Bild finde die zwei Worthälften.*

Beispiel 1 AF

A Brat	B saft	C Schasch	D dellen
E frites	F wurst	G Frika	H Schoko
I lade	J Apfel	K Pommes	L lik

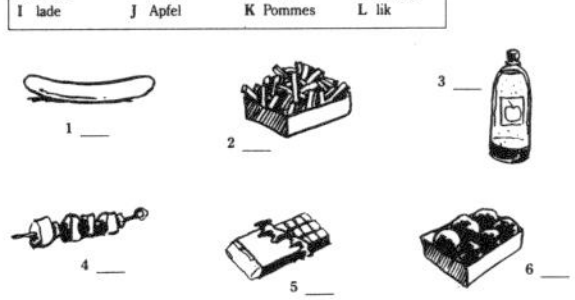

AT3 2

9B *Verbinde die Sätze und die Bilder.*

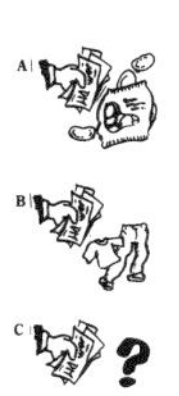

Ich kaufe mir Pommes frites.
Ich spare für Kleider.
Wofür gibst du dein Geld aus?
Ich kaufe mir Chips.
Wofür sparst du?
Ich gebe mein Geld für Kleider aus.

GLOSSARY

9A For each picture, find the two halves of the word.

9B Join the sentences and the pictures.

AT3 3

9C *Schreib den Dialog in der richtigen Reihenfolge.*

Beispiel F, …

A Möchtest du auch etwas zu trinken?
B Und ich nehme auch ein Erdbeereis.
C Ich auch! Gehen wir zur Eisbude?
D So, zweimal Erdbeereis, und ich nehme auch eine Cola. Was macht das?
E Ein Erdbeereis, bitte.
F Ich habe Hunger!
G Nein danke.
H Was nimmst du?

AT3 4

9D *Lies den Brief und die Sätze. Welche Sätze sind richtig (✔) und welche sind falsch (✗)?*

Beispiel
1 Werner ist in Bad Dürkheim. ✔

Lieber Nathan!
Grüße aus Bad Dürkheim! Ich verbringe ein paar Tage hier bei meinem Vater – es ist toll! Am Samstag waren wir in Kaiserslautern und haben das Fußballspiel gesehen. Heute nachmittag gehen wir in die Stadt, denn ich möchte Kleider kaufen. Nachher essen wir Eis – toll! Am Mittwoch gehen wir wahrscheinlich zum großen Jahrmarkt, also muß ich Geld dafür sparen, denn ich fahre sehr gern mit der Achterbahn!
Werner

1 Werner ist in Bad Dürkheim. ___
2 Er besucht seinen Großvater. ___
3 Er war am Sonntag in Kaiserslautern. ___
4 Heute kauft er Kleider. ___
5 Er ißt nicht gern Eis. ___
6 Er spart sein Geld für Kleider. ___
7 Der Jahrmarkt ist groß. ___
8 Werner möchte nicht mit der Achterbahn fahren. ___

GLOSSARY

9C Write the dialogue in the correct order.

9D Read the letter and the sentences. Which sentences are correct (✔) and which are incorrect (✗)?

AT4 1
AT3 2
AT4 2

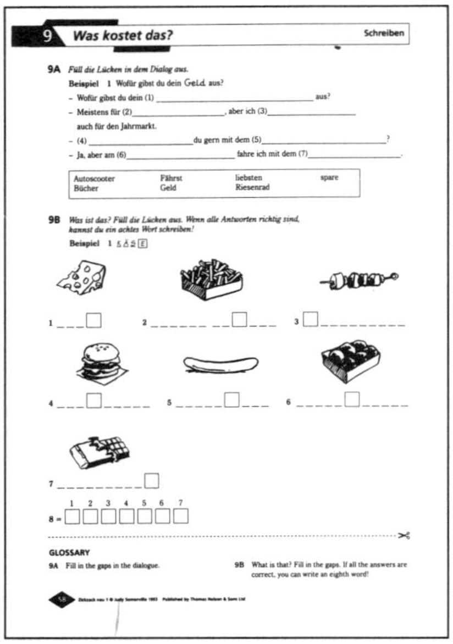

9 Was kostet das? — Schreiben

9A *Füll die Lücken in dem Dialog aus.*

Beispiel 1 Wofür gibst du dein Geld aus?

- Wofür gibst du dein (1) ________ aus?
- Meistens für (2) ________, aber ich (3) ________ auch für den Jahrmarkt.
- (4) ________ du gern mit dem (5) ________?
- Ja, aber am (6) ________ fahre ich mit dem (7) ________.

Autoscooter	Fährst	liebsten	spare
Bücher	Geld	Riesenrad	

9B *Was ist das? Füll die Lücken aus. Wenn alle Antworten richtig sind, kannst du ein achtes Wort schreiben!*

Beispiel 1 K Ä S [E]

1 _ _ _ ☐ 2 _ _ _ _ _ _ _ _ ☐ _ _ _ 3 ☐ _ _ _ _ _ _ _ _ _

4 _ _ _ ☐ _ _ _ _ _ 5 _ _ _ _ _ ☐ _ _ _ 6 _ _ _ _ _ ☐ _ _ _ _ _

7 _ _ _ _ _ _ _ _ _ ☐

8 = ☐ ☐ ☐ ☐ ☐ ☐ ☐ (1 2 3 4 5 6 7)

GLOSSARY

9A Fill in the gaps in the dialogue.

9B What is that? Fill in the gaps. If all the answers are correct, you can write an eighth word!

58 Zickzack neu 1 © Judy Somerville 1993 Published by Thomas Nelson & Sons Ltd

AT4 2
AT4 3

WAS KOSTET DAS? — Schreiben 9

9C *Sieh dir das Bild an. Schreib eine Einkaufsliste für den chaotischen Christof.*

Beispiel Chips

9D *Schreib einen Satz zu jedem Bild unten.*

Beispiel 1 Wofür sparst du?

1 ________ 2 ________

3 ________ 4 ________

5 ________ 6 ________

GLOSSARY

9C Look at the picture. Write a shopping list for chaotic Christof.

9D Write a sentence for each of the pictures below.

Zickzack neu 1 © Judy Somerville 1993 Published by Thomas Nelson & Sons Ltd 59

KAPITEL 10

AT1 1
AT1 2

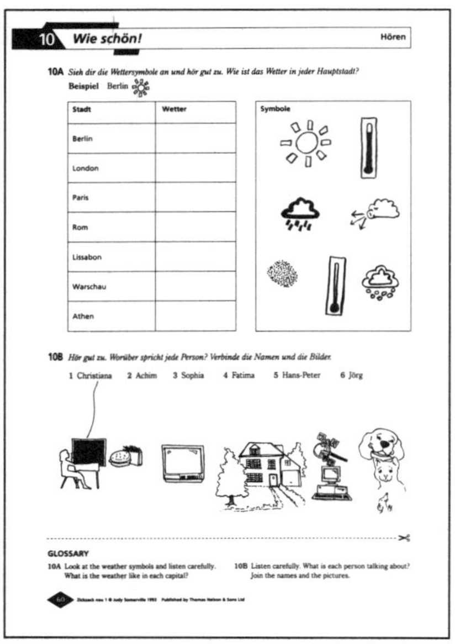

10 Wie schön! — Hören

10A *Sieh dir die Wettersymbole an und hör gut zu. Wie ist das Wetter in jeder Hauptstadt?*

Beispiel Berlin

Stadt	Wetter
Berlin	
London	
Paris	
Rom	
Lissabon	
Warschau	
Athen	

Symbole

10B *Hör gut zu. Worüber spricht jede Person? Verbinde die Namen und die Bilder.*

1 Christiana 2 Achim 3 Sophia 4 Fatima 5 Hans-Peter 6 Jörg

GLOSSARY

10A Look at the weather symbols and listen carefully. What is the weather like in each capital?

10B Listen carefully. What is each person talking about? Join the names and the pictures.

60 Zickzack neu 1 © Judy Somerville 1993 Published by Thomas Nelson & Sons Ltd

AT1 3
AT1 4

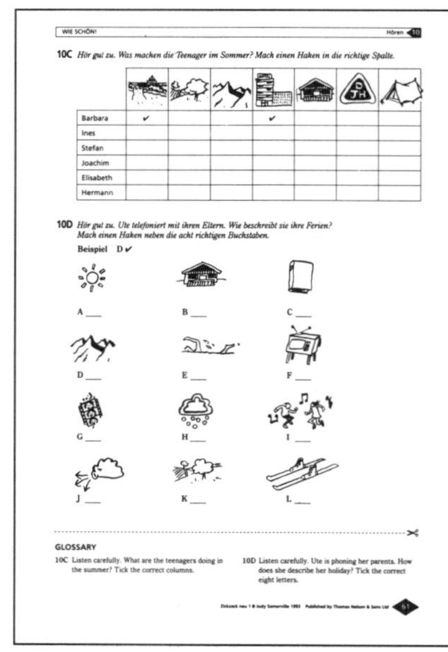

WIE SCHÖN! — Hören 10

10C *Hör gut zu. Was machen die Teenager im Sommer? Mach einen Haken in die richtige Spalte.*

Barbara	✔			✔			
Ines							
Stefan							
Joachim							
Elisabeth							
Hermann							

10D *Hör gut zu. Ute telefoniert mit ihren Eltern. Wie beschreibt sie ihre Ferien? Mach einen Haken neben die acht richtigen Buchstaben.*

Beispiel D ✔

A ___ B ___ C ___

D ___ E ___ F ___

G ___ H ___ I ___

J ___ K ___ L ___

GLOSSARY

10C Listen carefully. What are the teenagers doing in the summer? Tick the correct columns.

10D Listen carefully. Ute is phoning her parents. How does she describe her holiday? Tick the correct eight letters.

Zickzack neu 1 © Judy Somerville 1993 Published by Thomas Nelson & Sons Ltd 61

AT2 2
AT2 2

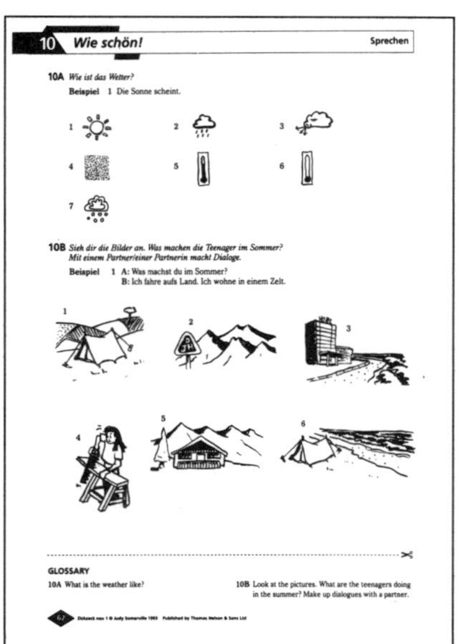

10 Wie schön! — Sprechen

10A *Wie ist das Wetter?*

Beispiel 1 Die Sonne scheint.

1 2 3 4 5 6 7

10B *Sieh dir die Bilder an. Was machen die Teenager im Sommer? Mit einem Partner/einer Partnerin macht Dialoge.*

Beispiel 1 A: Was machst du im Sommer?
B: Ich fahre aufs Land. Ich wohne in einem Zelt.

1 2 3 4 5 6

GLOSSARY

10A What is the weather like?

10B Look at the pictures. What are the teenagers doing in the summer? Make up dialogues with a partner.

62 Zickzack neu 1 © Judy Somerville 1993 Published by Thomas Nelson & Sons Ltd

AT2 4
AT1 2
AT2 4

WIE SCHÖN! — Sprechen 10

10C *Arbeitet zu zweit. Jede Person stellt vier Fragen über die Ferien. Die andere Person beantwortet die Fragen mit Hilfe der Bilder.*

Person A — Person B

Beispiel B: Wohin fährst du?
A: Ich fahre aufs Land.
B: Mit wem fährst du?
A: …

10D *Kannst du ungefähr 20–30 Sekunden lang über deine idealen Ferien sprechen? (Du darfst ein paar Notizen benutzen, wenn du willst.)*

Beispiel Ich fahre am liebsten nach Frankreich. Ich fahre mit meiner Familie ans Meer. Ich …

GLOSSARY

10C Work in a pair. Each person asks four questions about the holidays. The other person answers the questions with the help of the pictures.

10D Can you talk for about 20–30 seconds about your ideal holidays? (You can use a few notes if you wish.)

Zickzack neu 1 © Judy Somerville 1993 Published by Thomas Nelson & Sons Ltd 63

AT3 2

AT3 2, 3

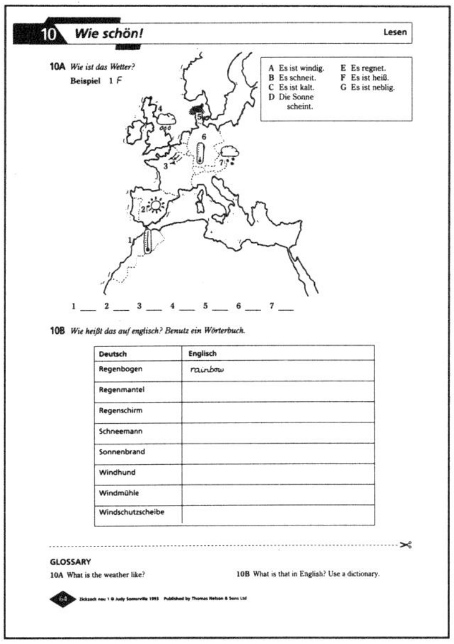

10 **Wie schön!** Lesen

10A *Wie ist das Wetter?*

Beispiel 1 F

A Es ist windig.
B Es schneit.
C Es ist kalt.
D Die Sonne scheint.
E Es regnet.
F Es ist heiß.
G Es ist neblig.

1 ___ 2 ___ 3 ___ 4 ___ 5 ___ 6 ___ 7 ___

10B *Wie heißt das auf englisch? Benutz ein Wörterbuch.*

Deutsch	Englisch
Regenbogen	rainbow
Regenmantel	
Regenschirm	
Schneemann	
Sonnenbrand	
Windhund	
Windmühle	
Windschutzscheibe	

GLOSSARY

10A What is the weather like?

10B What is that in English? Use a dictionary.

64 Zickzack neu 1 © Judy Somerville 1993 Published by Thomas Nelson & Sons Ltd

AT3 3

AT3 4

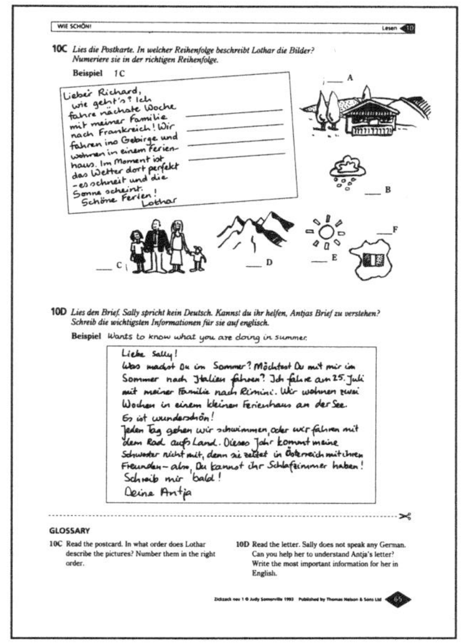

WIE SCHÖN! Lesen 10

10C *Lies die Postkarte. In welcher Reihenfolge beschreibt Lothar die Bilder? Numeriere sie in der richtigen Reihenfolge.*

Beispiel 1C

Lieber Richard,
wie geht's? Ich fahre nächste Woche mit meiner Familie nach Frankreich! Wir fahren ins Gebirge und wohnen in einem Ferienhaus. Im Moment ist das Wetter dort perfekt – es schneit und die Sonne scheint.
Schöne Ferien!
Lothar

___ A ___ B ___ C ___ D ___ E ___ F

10D *Lies den Brief. Sally spricht kein Deutsch. Kannst du ihr helfen, Antjas Brief zu verstehen? Schreib die wichtigsten Informationen für sie auf englisch.*

Beispiel Wants to know what you are doing in summer.

Liebe Sally!
Was machst Du im Sommer? Möchtest Du mit mir im Sommer nach Italien fahren? Ich fahre am 25. Juli mit meiner Familie nach Rimini. Wir wohnen zwei Wochen in einem kleinen Ferienhaus an der See. Es ist wunderschön!
Jeden Tag gehen wir schwimmen, oder wir fahren mit dem Rad aufs Land. Dieses Jahr kommt meine Schwester nicht mit, denn sie zeltet in Österreich mit ihren Freunden – also, Du kannst ihr Schlafzimmer haben!
Schreib mir bald!
Deine Antja

GLOSSARY

10C Read the postcard. In what order does Lothar describe the pictures? Number them in the right order.

10D Read the letter. Sally does not speak any German. Can you help her to understand Antja's letter? Write the most important information for her in English.

Zickzack neu 1 © Judy Somerville 1993 Published by Thomas Nelson & Sons Ltd 65

AT4 1,2
AT3 2

AT4 2

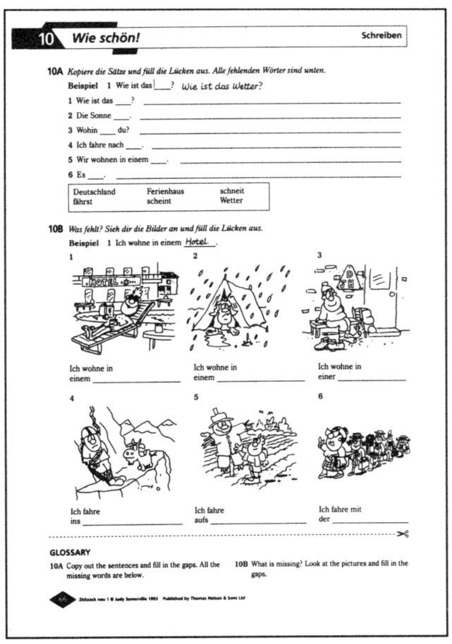

10 **Wie schön!** Schreiben

10A *Kopiere die Sätze und füll die Lücken aus. Alle fehlenden Wörter sind unten.*

Beispiel 1 Wie ist das ___? Wie ist das Wetter?

1 Wie ist das ___?
2 Die Sonne ___.
3 Wohin ___ du?
4 Ich fahre nach ___.
5 Wir wohnen in einem ___.
6 Es ___.

Deutschland, fährst, Ferienhaus, scheint, schneit, Wetter

10B *Was fehlt? Sieh dir die Bilder an und füll die Lücken aus.*

Beispiel 1 Ich wohne in einem Hotel.

1 Ich wohne in einem ______
2 Ich wohne in einem ______
3 Ich wohne in einer ______
4 Ich fahre ins ______
5 Ich fahre aufs ______
6 Ich fahre mit der ______

GLOSSARY

10A Copy out the sentences and fill in the gaps. All the missing words are below.

10B What is missing? Look at the pictures and fill in the gaps.

66 Zickzack neu 1 © Judy Somerville 1993 Published by Thomas Nelson & Sons Ltd

AT4 3
AT3 2

AT4 4
AT3 3

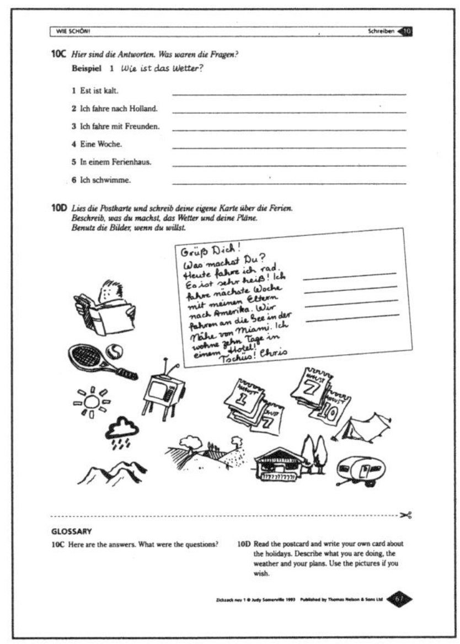

WIE SCHÖN! Schreiben 10

10C *Hier sind die Antworten. Was waren die Fragen?*

Beispiel 1 Wie ist das Wetter?

1 Est ist kalt.
2 Ich fahre nach Holland.
3 Ich fahre mit Freunden.
4 Eine Woche.
5 In einem Ferienhaus.
6 Ich schwimme.

10D *Lies die Postkarte und schreib deine eigene Karte über die Ferien. Beschreib, was du machst, das Wetter und deine Pläne. Benutz die Bilder, wenn du willst.*

Grüß Dich!
Was machst Du? Heute fahre ich rad. Es ist sehr heiß! Ich fahre nächste Woche mit meinen Eltern nach Amerika. Wir fahren an die See in der Nähe von Miami. Ich wohne zehn Tage in einem Hotel!
Tschüs! Chris

GLOSSARY

10C Here are the answers. What were the questions?

10D Read the postcard and write your own card about the holidays. Describe what you are doing, the weather and your plans. Use the pictures if you wish.

Zickzack neu 1 © Judy Somerville 1993 Published by Thomas Nelson & Sons Ltd 67

ABSCHLUSSTEST

AT1 1

AT1 1

AT1 2

Abschlußtest (Kapitel 1–10) — Hören

A *Hör gut zu. Welches Bild ist das?*

Beispiel 1 A

A B C D E F

1 ___ 2 ___ 3 ___ 4 ___ 5 ___ 6 ___

B *Hör gut zu. Schreib die Lottonummern in der richtigen Reihenfolge.*

Beispiel 29, ...

12	29	47	74
13	30	54	86
21	45	68	92

C *Worüber sprechen die Teenager? Hör gut zu und mach einen Haken (✔) in die richtige Spalte.*

	Name	Wohnort	Familie	Haustiere	Hobbys
1	Dieter	✔			
2	Susi				
3	Alexandra				
4	Yusuf				
5	Nicole				

GLOSSARY

A Listen carefully. Which picture is that?
B Listen carefully. Write the Bingo numbers in the correct order.
C What are the teenagers talking about? Listen carefully and tick the correct column.

68 Zickzack neu 1 © Judy Somerville 1993 Published by Thomas Nelson & Sons Ltd

AT1 2

AT1 3
AT3 2

AT1 3

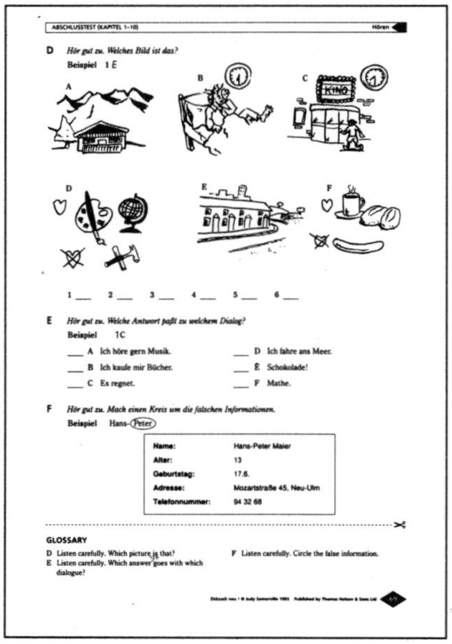

ABSCHLUSSTEST (KAPITEL 1–10) Hören

D *Hör gut zu. Welches Bild ist das?*

Beispiel 1 E

1 ___ 2 ___ 3 ___ 4 ___ 5 ___ 6 ___

E *Hör gut zu. Welche Antwort paßt zu welchem Dialog?*

Beispiel 1C

___ A Ich höre gern Musik.
___ B Ich kaufe mir Bücher.
___ C Es regnet.
___ D Ich fahre ans Meer.
___ E Schokolade!
___ F Mathe.

F *Hör gut zu. Mach einen Kreis um die falschen Informationen.*

Beispiel Hans-(Peter)

Name:	Hans-Peter Maier
Alter:	13
Geburtstag:	17.6.
Adresse:	Mozartstraße 45, Neu-Ulm
Telefonnummer:	94 32 68

GLOSSARY

D Listen carefully. Which picture is that?
E Listen carefully. Which answer goes with which dialogue?
F Listen carefully. Circle the false information.

Zickzack neu 1 © Judy Somerville 1993 Published by Thomas Nelson & Sons Ltd 69

AT2 1

AT2 2

AT2 3,4
AT1 2

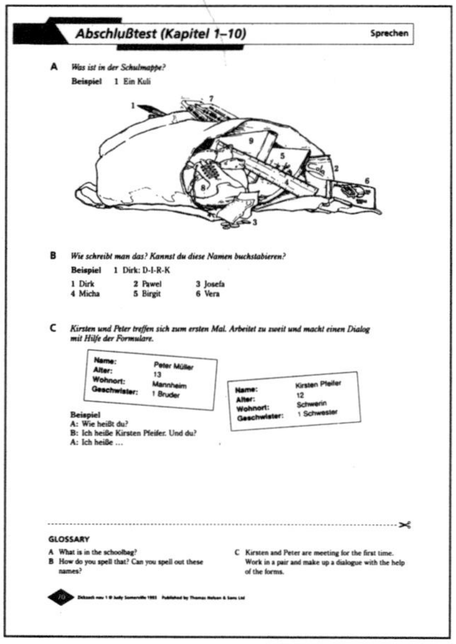

Abschlußtest (Kapitel 1–10) — Sprechen

A *Was ist in der Schulmappe?*

Beispiel 1 Ein Kuli

B *Wie schreibt man das? Kannst du diese Namen buchstabieren?*

Beispiel 1 Dirk: D-I-R-K

1 Dirk 2 Pawel 3 Josefa
4 Micha 5 Birgit 6 Vera

C *Kirsten und Peter treffen sich zum ersten Mal. Arbeitet zu zweit und macht einen Dialog mit Hilfe der Formulare.*

Name:	Peter Müller
Alter:	13
Wohnort:	Mannheim
Geschwister:	1 Bruder

Name:	Kirsten Pfeifer
Alter:	12
Wohnort:	Schwerin
Geschwister:	1 Schwester

Beispiel
A: Wie heißt du?
B: Ich heiße Kirsten Pfeifer. Und du?
A: Ich heiße ...

GLOSSARY

A What is in the schoolbag?
B How do you spell that? Can you spell out these names?
C Kirsten and Peter are meeting for the first time. Work in a pair and make up a dialogue with the help of the forms.

70 Zickzack neu 1 © Judy Somerville 1993 Published by Thomas Nelson & Sons Ltd

AT2 4,5
AT1 2

AT2 4
AT3 1

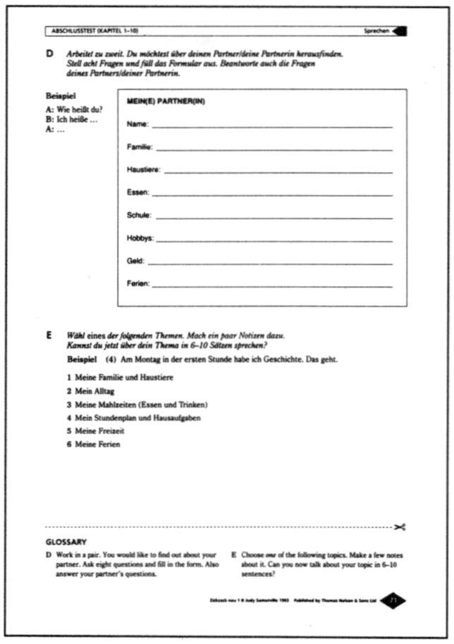

ABSCHLUSSTEST (KAPITEL 1–10) Sprechen

D *Arbeitet zu zweit. Du möchtest über deinen Partner/deine Partnerin herausfinden. Stell acht Fragen und füll das Formular aus. Beantworte auch die Fragen deines Partners/deiner Partnerin.*

Beispiel
A: Wie heißt du?
B: Ich heiße ...
A: ...

MEIN(E) PARTNER(IN)

Name: ____________
Familie: ____________
Haustiere: ____________
Essen: ____________
Schule: ____________
Hobbys: ____________
Geld: ____________
Ferien: ____________

E *Wähl* eines *der folgenden Themen. Mach ein paar Notizen dazu. Kannst du jetzt über dein Thema in 6–10 Sätzen sprechen?*

Beispiel (4) Am Montag in der ersten Stunde habe ich Geschichte. Das geht.

1 Meine Familie und Haustiere
2 Mein Alltag
3 Meine Mahlzeiten (Essen und Trinken)
4 Mein Stundenplan und Hausaufgaben
5 Meine Freizeit
6 Meine Ferien

GLOSSARY

D Work in a pair. You would like to find out about your partner. Ask eight questions and fill in the form. Also answer your partner's questions.
E Choose *one* of the following topics. Make a few notes about it. Can you now talk about your topic in 6–10 sentences?

Zickzack neu 1 © Judy Somerville 1993 Published by Thomas Nelson & Sons Ltd 71

AT3 1

AT3 2

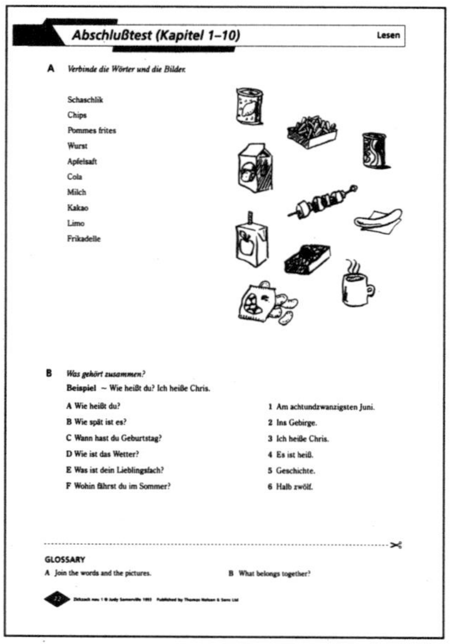

Abschlußtest (Kapitel 1–10) — Lesen

A *Verbinde die Wörter und die Bilder.*

Schaschlik
Chips
Pommes frites
Wurst
Apfelsaft
Cola
Milch
Kakao
Limo
Frikadelle

B *Was gehört zusammen?*

Beispiel – Wie heißt du? Ich heiße Chris.

A Wie heißt du? — 1 Am achtundzwanzigsten Juni.
B Wie spät ist es? — 2 Ins Gebirge.
C Wann hast du Geburtstag? — 3 Ich heiße Chris.
D Wie ist das Wetter? — 4 Es ist heiß.
E Was ist dein Lieblingsfach? — 5 Geschichte.
F Wohin fährst du im Sommer? — 6 Halb zwölf.

GLOSSARY

A Join the words and the pictures.
B What belongs together?

72 Zickzack neu 1 © Judy Somerville 1993 Published by Thomas Nelson & Sons Ltd

AT3 2,3

AT3 2

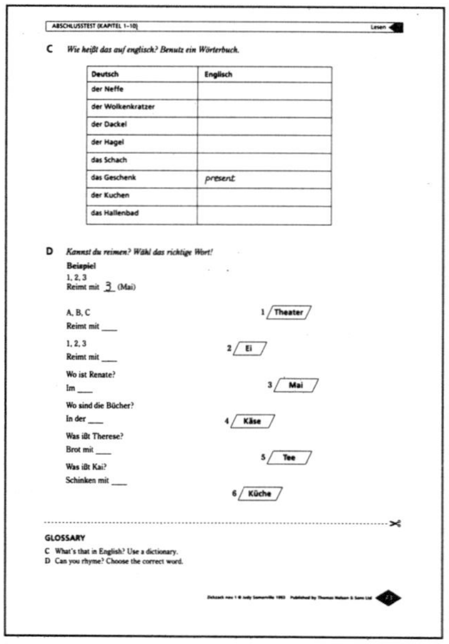

ABSCHLUSSTEST (KAPITEL 1–10) Lesen

C *Wie heißt das auf englisch? Benutz ein Wörterbuch.*

Deutsch	Englisch
der Neffe	
der Wolkenkratzer	
der Dackel	
der Hagel	
das Schach	
das Geschenk	present
der Kuchen	
das Hallenbad	

D *Kannst du reimen? Wähl das richtige Wort!*

Beispiel
1, 2, 3
Reimt mit 3 (Mai)

A, B, C
Reimt mit ___

1, 2, 3
Reimt mit ___

Wo ist Renate?
Im ___

Wo sind die Bücher?
In der ___

Was ißt Therese?
Brot mit ___

Was ißt Kai?
Schinken mit ___

1 Theater
2 Ei
3 Mai
4 Käse
5 Tee
6 Küche

GLOSSARY

C What's that in English? Use a dictionary.
D Can you rhyme? Choose the correct word.

Zickzack neu 1 © Judy Somerville 1993 Published by Thomas Nelson & Sons Ltd 73

AT3 3

AT3 3

ABSCHLUSSTEST (KAPITEL 1–10) Lesen

E *Lies die Texte und die Sätze. Welche Sätze sind richtig (✔) und welche sind falsch (✗)?*

Beispiel 1 ✗

1 Mathe ist langweilig! Kommst du nach der Schule in die Stadt? Paul

2 Ich gehe mit dem Hund spazieren. Ich bin um 4.00 wieder zu Hause. Tanja

3 Was machst du heute Abend? Ich fahre rad. Kommst du mit? Jens

4 Der Film beginnt um 7.30. Ich treffe dich um 7.15 im Kino. Sonja.

5 Das Fußballspiel beginnt um 2.15. Kommst du mit? Wir verlassen das Haus um 1.45. Max

1 Mathe gefällt Paul. ___

2 Tanja bleibt zu Hause. ___

3 Jens fährt rad. ___

4 Der Film beginnt um halb acht. ___

5 Max verläßt das Haus um Viertel vor zwei. ___

F *Numeriere die Sätze in der richtigen Reihenfolge.*

Beispiel D 1

A Ich frühstücke. ___
B Ich gehe nach Hause und esse mein Mittagessen. ___
C In der ersten Stunde habe ich Deutsch. ___
D Es ist halb sieben. ___
E Ich verlasse das Haus. ___
F Die Schule endet um Viertel vor eins. ___
G Ich stehe auf. ___
H Ich gehe in die Schule. ___

GLOSSARY

E Read the texts and the sentences. Which sentences are correct (✔) and which are wrong (✗)?

F Number the sentences in the correct order.

74 Zickzack neu 1 © Judy Somerville 1993 Published by Thomas Nelson & Sons Ltd

AT3 5

ABSCHLUSSTEST (KAPITEL 1–10) Lesen

G *Lies den Brief. Numeriere die Bilder in der richtigen Reihenfolge.*

Beispiel G 1

Greifswald, den 3. Juli

Liebe Claire!

Meine Englischlehrerin hat mir Deinen Namen gegeben, denn ich möchte eine englische Brieffreundin. Ich bin dreizehn Jahre alt und wohne in Greifswald, im Nordosten von Deutschland. Ich habe einen Bruder – er ist elf Jahre alt und heißt Thomas. Wir haben einen Hund und ein Kaninchen. In meiner Freizeit fahre ich gern rad, ich lese und ich gehe mit dem Hund spazieren. Nächste Woche beginnen die Ferien, und ich fahre mit meiner Familie ins Gebirge, aber ab 23. Juli bin ich wieder zu Hause. Hoffentlich willst Du meine Brieffreundin werden – ich freue mich auf einen Brief oder eine Postkarte!

Viele Grüße

Deine Nicole

GLOSSARY

G Read the letter. Number the pictures in the correct order.

Zickzack neu 1 © Judy Somerville 1993 Published by Thomas Nelson & Sons Ltd 75

AT4 1

AT4 2
AT3 2

Abschlußtest (Kapitel 1–10) Schreiben

A *Sieh dir das Bild und die Wörter an. Welches Wort gehört zu welcher Nummer?*

Beispiel 1 der Tisch

1 ______ 5 ______
2 ______ 6 ______
3 ______ 7 ______
4 ______ 8 ______

das Bett
die Bücher
der Goldfisch
das Heft
der Hund
der Kuli
der Tisch
die Turnschuhe

B *Füll die Lücken aus.*

Beispiel Wie heißt du?

1 Wie ______ du?
2 Wohnst du ______?
3 ______ Fußball?
4 ______ nicht gern?
5 Was ist ______?
6 Was machst du ______?

Spielst du gern / in deiner Freizeit? / dein Lieblingsfach? / in der Stadtmitte? / Was ißt du / heißt

GLOSSARY

A Look at the picture and the words. Which word belongs with which number?

B Fill in the gaps.

76 Zickzack neu 1 © Judy Somerville 1993 Published by Thomas Nelson & Sons Ltd

AT4 2
AT3 1

AT4 2

ABSCHLUSSTEST (KAPITEL 1–10) Schreiben

C *Schreib die Wörter in der richtigen Reihenfolge.*

Beispiel 1 Ich heiße Jo.

1 heiße Jo Ich. ______
2 alt bist Wie du? ______
3 einen habe Bruder Ich. ______
4 trinke Apfelsaft Ich gern. ______
5 spät ist Wie es? ______
6 Lieblingsfach Geschichte ist Mein. ______

D *Füll das Rätsel aus.*

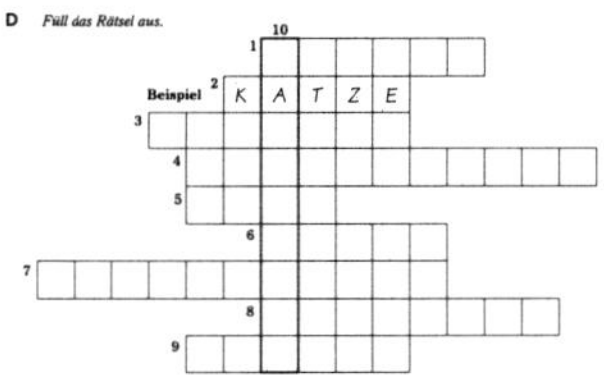

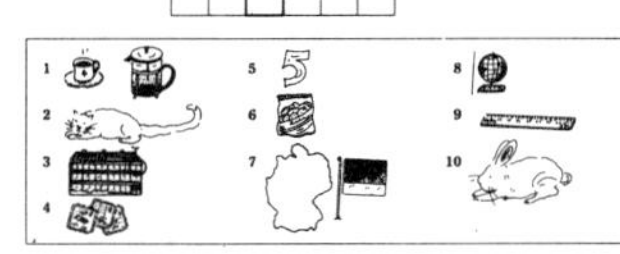

GLOSSARY

C Write the words in the correct order.

D Fill in the puzzle.

Zickzack neu 1 © Judy Somerville 1993 Published by Thomas Nelson & Sons Ltd 77

AT4 3

AT4 3
AT3 2

AT4 4,5

ABSCHLUSSTEST (KAPITEL 1–10) Schreiben

E *Wie ist das Wetter?*

Beispiel 1 Es ist windig.

F *Hier sind die Antworten. Was waren die Fragen?*

Beispiel 1 Wie heißt du? Ich heiße Helena.

1 ______ Ich heiße Helena.
2 ______ Ich habe einen Hamster.
3 ______ An meinem Geburtstag gehe ich ins Kino.
4 ______ Ich habe Deutsch in der ersten Stunde.
5 ______ Ich spare für ein Rad.
6 ______ Ich fahre mit Freunden nach Irland.

G *Schreib einen kurzen Brief an einem/einer deutschsprachigen Brieffreund(in). Schreib etwas über dich, deine Familie und Haustiere, deine Freizeit und deine Sommerferien.*

GLOSSARY

E What is the weather like?

F Here are the answers. What were the questions?

G Write a short letter to a German-speaking penfriend. Write something about yourself, your family and pets, your free time and your summer holidays.

78 Zickzack neu 1 © Judy Somerville 1993 Published by Thomas Nelson & Sons Ltd

1 Hallo! Wie heißt du?

Hören 1A

Hallo! Ich heiße Thomas.
Tag! Ich heiße Melanie.
Ich bin Tamara.
Hallo! Ich heiße Christof.
Grüß dich! Ich bin Karl-Heinz.
Tag! Ich heiße Anneli.

Hören 1B

1 – So, Kerstin. Wie schreibt man das?
– K-E-R-S-T-I-N.
2 – Wie schreibt man „Nathalie" bitte?
– N-A-T-H-A-L-I-E.
3 – Ich heiße Lydia: L-Y-D-I-A.
4 – Fritjof? Wie schreibt man das?
– F-R-I-T-J-O-F.
5 – Ich heiße Wazlav: W-A-Z-L-A-V.

Hören 1C

1 drei
2 zehn
3 null
4 sieben
5 acht
6 fünf

Hören 1D

1 Hallo. Ich heiße Heidi. Ich bin elf Jahre alt.
2 Grüß dich. Mein Name ist Stefan. Ich bin vierzehn.
3 Guten Tag! Ich heiße Ute. Ich bin zwölf.
4 Hallo! Ich heiße Joachim. Ich bin sieben Jahre alt.
5 Tag! Ich bin fünfzehn Jahre alt. Ich heiße Christiane.
6 Grüß dich. Ich heiße Adam. Ich bin zehn.

Sprechen 1A

1 das Heft
2 der Tisch
3 der Stuhl
4 der Kuli
5 die Mappe
6 die Tür

Sprechen 1B

Beispiel
Journalistin: Guten Tag.
Du: Guten Tag.
Journalistin: Wie heißt du?
Du: Ich heiße Jo.
Journalistin: Wie schreibt man das?
Du: J-O
Journalistin: Wie alt bist du?
Du: Ich bin zwölf Jahre alt.

Sprechen 1C

Beispiel
Maria: Wie heißt du?
Achim: Ich heiße Achim. Und du?
Maria: Ich heiße Maria.
Achim: Wie alt bist du?
Maria: Ich bin elf Jahre alt. Wie alt bist du?
Achim: Ich bin zwölf.

2 Wo wohnst du?

Hören 2A

1 Ich heiße Anja, und ich komme aus Deutschland.
2 Ich heiße Axel, und ich komme aus der Schweiz.
3 Ich heiße Elisabeth, und ich komme aus Dänemark.
4 Ich heiße Yannick, und ich komme aus Frankreich.
5 Ich heiße Marie, und ich komme aus Belgien.
6 Ich heiße Thorsten, und ich komme aus Österreich.

Hören 2B

1 Ich heiße Tobias. Ich komme aus Deutschland. Ich wohne in Stuttgart.
2 Ich heiße Bärbel. Ich wohne in Hamburg, in Deutschland.
3 Mein Name ist Peter. Ich komme aus Österreich. Ich wohne in Wien.
4 Ich heiße Monika. Ich komme aus Deutschland. Ich wohne in Schwerin.
5 Ich heiße Christel. Ich komme aus Österreich. Ich wohne in Salzburg.
6 Mein Name ist Hans. Ich wohne in Hannover, in Deutschland.

Hören 2C

1 Ich wohne in Aachen, im Westen.
2 Ich wohne in Cottbus, im Osten.
3 Ich wohne in Füssen. Das liegt im Süden.
4 Ich wohne in Flensburg, im Norden.
5 Ich wohne in Krefeld. Das liegt im Westen.
6 Ich wohne in Kempten, im Süden.
7 Ich wohne in Eisenhüttenstadt. Das liegt im Osten.
8 Ich wohne in Lübeck, im Norden.

Sprechen 2A

1 Ich komme aus England.
2 Ich komme aus Frankreich.
3 Ich komme aus Deutschland.
4 Ich komme aus Dänemark.
5 Ich komme aus Schottland.
6 Ich komme aus Irland.
7 Ich komme aus Wales.
8 Ich komme aus Italien.

Sprechen 2B

1 Ich heiße Erik. Ich komme aus Deutschland. Ich wohne in Hamburg. Das liegt im Norden.

2 Ich heiße Uschi. Ich komme aus Deutschland. Ich wohne in Berlin. Das liegt im Osten.
3 Ich heiße Lars. Ich komme aus Österreich. Ich wohne in Wien. Das liegt im Norden.
4 Ich heiße Kai. Ich komme aus Deutschland. Ich wohne in München. Das liegt im Süden.
5 Ich heiße Susi. Ich komme aus der Schweiz. Ich wohne in Zürich. Das liegt im Norden.
6 Ich heiße Ute. Ich komme aus Deutschland. Ich wohne in Köln. Das liegt im Westen.

Sprechen 2C

Beispiel
Ich heiße Jo.
Ich komme aus Wales.
Ich wohne in Cardiff.
Das liegt im Süden.

3 Meine Familie

Hören 3A

Ich heiße Steffi. Ich habe einen Fisch.
Ich heiße Britta. Ich habe ein Pferd.
Ich heiße Michael. Ich habe einen Hund.
Ich heiße Lars. Ich habe eine Katze.
Ich heiße Julia. Ich habe eine Maus.
Ich heiße Niko. Ich habe ein Kaninchen.

Hören 3B

1 Ich habe eine kleine schwarze Katze.
2 Ich habe ein braunes Kaninchen, das Boris heißt.
3 Ich habe einen älteren Bruder.
4 Ich habe zwei jüngere Geschwister, Markus und Oliver.
5 Ich habe einen großen schwarzen Schäferhund.
6 Ich habe viele tropische Fische und ein kleines Meerschweinchen.

Hören 3C

Ich heiße Micha. Ich habe einen Bruder und eine Schwester.
Ich heiße Elena. Ich habe zwei Schwestern.
Ich heiße Nadine. Ich bin ein Einzelkind.
Ich heiße Johann. Ich habe zwei Brüder und eine Schwester.
Ich heiße Jasmin. Ich habe drei Schwestern und einen Bruder.
Ich heiße Richard. Ich habe einen Bruder.

Sprechen 3A

1 **A:** Was ist das?
B: Das ist ein Hund.
2 **A:** Was ist das?
B: Das ist eine Katze.
3 **A:** Was ist das?
B: Das ist eine Maus.
4 **A:** Was ist das?
B: Das ist ein Kaninchen.
5 **A:** Was ist das?
B: Das ist ein Pferd.
6 **A:** Was ist das?
B: Das ist ein Meerschweinchen.

Sprechen 3B

1 Ich heiße Paul. Ich habe eine Schwester.
2 Ich heiße Sabine. Ich habe einen Bruder.
3 Ich heiße Andreas. Ich habe eine Katze und einen Hund.
4 Ich heiße Marion. Ich habe zwei Brüder und ein Kaninchen.
5 Ich heiße Jutta. Ich bin ein Einzelkind, und ich habe ein Pferd.
6 Ich heiße Raphael. Ich habe zwei Schwestern und einen Hamster.

Sprechen 3C

1 – Wie heißt du?
– Ich heiße Susanne.
2 – Wo wohnst du?
– Ich wohne in Wien.
3 – Wie alt bist du?
– Ich bin zwölf Jahre alt.
4 – Hast du Geschwister?
– Nein. Ich bin Einzelkind.
5 – Hast du ein Haustier?
– Ja. Ich habe ein Meerschweinchen.

Sprechen 3D

Beispiel
– Wie heißt du?
– Ich heiße Jo.
– Wie alt bist du?
– Ich bin elf Jahre alt.
– Hast du Geschwister?
– Ich habe einen Bruder und eine Schwester.
– Hast du ein Haustier?
– Ja, ich habe eine Katze.

4 Bei mir zu Hause

Hören 4A

1 – Dieter, wie ist deine Adresse?
– Hauptstraße 78.
2 – Wie ist deine Adresse, Sara?
– Also, Rheinstraße 51.
3 – Wo wohnst du, Nils?
– Zum Sandweg 24.
4 – Und du, Nina – wie ist deine Adresse?
– Sommergasse 32.
5 – Wie ist deine Adresse, Josef?
– Bergmannstraße 96.
6 – Und du, Heidi – wie ist deine Adresse?
– Am Marktplatz 45.

Hören 4B

1 Interviewer: Wie ist deine Telefonnummer, Erich?
Erich: 56 19 24
2 Interviewer: Kerstin, wie ist deine Telefonnummer?
Kerstin: 31 48 60
3 – 42 ... 98 ... 20
– Meyer.
– Hallo Ingrid, wie geht's?
4 So, Peter Müller ... Telefonnummer 73 ... 85 ... 11.

5 – 51 ... 27 ... 64
– Santos.
– Tag Fatima, wie geht's?
6 **Interviewer:** Martin, wie ist deine Telefonnummer?
Martin: 37 15 90

Hören 4C

1 Ich wohne in Mörsch, einem Dorf in der Nähe von Frankenthal. Wir haben einen Bungalow. Er ist schön und groß mit sechs Zimmern.
2 Wir haben ein Reihenhaus. Es ist in der Stadtmitte. Wir haben keine Garage.
3 Ich wohne in der Stadtmitte. Wir haben eine kleine drei-Zimmer-Wohnung.
4 Ich wohne in der Dorfmitte. Wir haben ein großes altes Bauernhaus.
5 Ich wohne am Stadtrand. Wir haben eine schöne moderne Wohnung.
6 Wir haben ein Einfamilienhaus am Stadtrand. Es hat fünf Zimmer. Ich teile mein Zimmer mit meiner Schwester.

Hören 4D

1 So ... ich zeige dir die Zimmer. Das hier ist das Wohnzimmer ... und hier ist das Eßzimmer ... Und dein Zimmer ist hier.
2 Wir haben ein großes Haus mit einem Keller und einer Garage. Das Wohnzimmer ist schön und groß.
3 So: hier ist dein Zimmer. Und das Badezimmer ist hier. Meine Mutter ist im Wohnzimmer, wenn du fertig bist.
4 Wir haben eine kleine Wohnung mit zwei Schlafzimmern, Wohnzimmer, Küche und Badezimmer.
5 So: hier ist die Toilette ... und das Wohnzimmer ... Dein Zimmer ist oben.

Sprechen 4A

Martina Becker: ein Meter einundneunzig.
Gabi Schwarz: ein Meter dreiundsiebzig.
Anna Heilmann: ein Meter fünfundachtzig.
Steffi Risch: ein Meter achtundsechzig.
Marion Jurek: ein Meter siebenundachtzig.
Sandra Palm: ein Meter neunundvierzig.

Sprechen 4B

Hier ist das Eßzimmer.
Hier ist die Küche.
Hier ist das Wohnzimmer.
Hier ist der Keller.
Hier ist mein Zimmer.
Hier ist das Schlafzimmer von meinen Eltern.
Hier ist das Badezimmer.
Hier ist die Toilette.

Sprechen 4C

1 **A:** Wie heißt du?
B: Ich heiße Tanja Dennen.
A: Wie ist deine Adresse?
B: Meine Adresse ist Schulstraße 21.
A: Wie ist deine Telefonnummer?
B: Meine Telefonnummer ist 71 14 02.
2 **A:** Wie heißt du?
B: Ich heiße Tamara Englert.
A: Wie ist deine Adresse?
B: Meine Adresse ist Hauptstraße 12.
A: Wie ist deine Telefonnummer?
B: Meine Telefonnummer ist 62 11.
3 **A:** Wie heißt du?
B: Ich heiße Andreas Fischer.
A: Wie ist deine Adresse?
B: Meine Adresse ist Friedrichstraße 83.
A: Wie ist deine Telefonnummer?
B: Meine Telefonnummer ist 67 41 08.
4 **A:** Wie heißt du?
B: Ich heiße Paul Kempf.
A: Wie ist deine Adresse?
B: Meine Adresse ist Lindenstraße 36.
A: Wie ist deine Telefonnummer?
B: Meine Telefonnummer ist 47 22 66.
5 **A:** Wie heißt du?
B: Ich heiße Silke Tast.
A: Wie ist deine Adresse?
B: Meine Adresse ist Gartenstraße 52.
A: Wie ist deine Telefonnummer?
B: Meine Telefonnummer ist 15 85.
6 **A:** Wie heißt du?
B: Ich heiße Christian Werner.
A: Wie ist deine Adresse?
B: Meine Adresse ist Hermannstraße 28.
A: Wie ist deine Telefonnummer?
B: Meine Telefonnummer ist 91 28 35.

Sprechen 4D

1 **A:** Wo wohnst du?
B: Ich wohne in der Stadtmitte. Wir haben ein Haus.
2 **A:** Wo wohnst du?
B: Ich wohne in einem Dorf. Wir haben einen Bungalow.
3 **A:** Wo wohnst du?
B: Ich wohne in der Stadmitte. Wir haben eine Wohnung.
4 **A:** Wo wohnst du?
B: Ich wohne am Stadtrand. Wir haben ein Haus.
5 **A:** Wo wohnst du?
B: Ich wohne in der Stadtmitte. Wir haben ein Reihenhaus.
6 **A:** Wo wohnst du?
B: Ich wohne am Stadtrand. Wir haben eine Wohnung.

Schreiben 4B

– Wo wohnst du?
– Ich wohne in einem Dorf. Wir haben ein Einfamilienhaus. Es ist ganz alt, und wir haben sechs Zimmer. Meine Adresse ist Mozartweg 6.

5 Mein Alltag

Hören 5A

1 – Wie spät ist es?
– Es ist zwei Uhr.

2 – Wie spät ist es?
– Viertel vor fünf.
3 – Wieviel Uhr ist es?
– Es ist halb sieben.
4 – Wie spät ist es?
– Zehn nach neun.
5 – Wie spät ist es?
– Fünfundzwanzig vor drei.
6 – Wieviel Uhr ist es?
– Es ist Viertel vor zwölf.
7 – Wie spät ist es?
– Halb zehn.
8 – Wie spät ist es?
– Fünf vor acht.
9 – Wieviel Uhr ist es?
– Es ist zwanzig nach vier.

Hören 5B

– Ich heiße Jens. Ich habe am 14. April Geburtstag.
– Ich heiße Jutta. Ich habe am 4. Oktober Geburtstag.
– Ich heiße Markus. Ich habe am 22. März Geburtstag.
– Ich heiße Alexander. Ich habe am 23. Juli Geburtstag.
– Ich heiße Petra. Ich habe am 6. August Geburtstag.
– Ich heiße Oliver. Ich habe am 19. Februar Geburtstag.
– Ich heiße Brigitte. Ich habe am 16. September Geburtstag.
– Ich heiße Nadine. Ich habe am 31. Mai Geburtstag.

Hören 5C

1 So ... *Formel eins* am 27. Mai um Viertel vor eins.
2 Jetzt ... *Guten Morgen* ... am 28. Mai. Das ist um halb acht.
3 *Horoskop.* Oh ja! Am 31. Mai – an meinem Geburtstag – um fünfundzwanzig nach neun.
4 Also ... *Yogi Bär* am 1. Juni um fünf vor zehn.
5 Toll! *Raumschiff Enterprise* am 3. Juni um zwanzig nach elf.
6 Oh ja ... und Tennis in *Sport extra* am 17. Juni. Das ist um Viertel nach zwölf.

Hören 5D

1 – Was machst du heute abend, Anna?
– Nichts Besonderes! Ich sehe fern und gehe ins Bett.
2 – Ralf, was machst du?
– Meine Hausaufgaben!
3 – Kasimir, was machst du heute abend?
– Ich esse, und dann treffe ich mich mit meinen Freunden.
4 – Machst du deine Hausaufgaben, Sabine?
– Nein! Ich gehe in die Stadt und treffe mich mit Freunden.
5 – Kommst du in die Stadt, Dorit?
– Nein. Ich bin krank. Ich gehe ins Bett.
6 – Was machst du heute abend, Werner?
– Ich mache meine Hausaufgaben und sehe fern.

Sprechen 5A

1 Es ist sieben Uhr.
2 Es ist Viertel nach drei.
3 Es ist zwanzig nach neun.
4 Es ist Viertel vor sieben.
5 Es ist fünfundzwanzig vor eins.
6 Es ist halb acht.
7 Es ist zehn vor vier.
8 Es ist fünf nach zwei.
9 Es ist halb zwölf.

Sprechen 5B

Es ist Viertel vor zwei. Ich stehe auf.
Es ist Viertel nach drei. Ich sehe fern.
Es ist halb sechs. Ich esse.
Es ist fünfundzwanzig nach sieben. Ich verlasse das Haus.
Es ist acht Uhr. Ich treffe mich mit Freunden.
Es ist zehn nach vier. Ich gehe ins Bett.

Sprechen 5C

1 **A:** Wann hast du Geburtstag?
B: Ich habe am 14. März Geburtstag.
2 **B:** Wann hast du Geburtstag?
A: Ich habe am 24. Oktober Geburtstag.
3 **A:** Wann hast du Geburtstag?
B: Ich habe am 29. Juni Geburtstag.
4 **B:** Wann hast du Geburtstag?
A: Ich habe am 2. September Geburtstag.
5 **A:** Wann hast du Geburtstag?
B: Ich habe am 7. Januar Geburtstag.
6 **B:** Wann hast du Geburtstag?
A: Ich habe am 1. Mai Geburtstag.

Sprechen 5D

Beispiel
Ich stehe um Viertel vor sieben auf.
Ich wasche mich um zehn vor sieben.
Ich frühstücke um sieben Uhr.
Ich sehe um Viertel nach sieben fern.
Ich verlasse das Haus um halb acht.
Ich treffe mich mit meinen Freunden um fünf nach acht.

6 *Wie schmeckt's?*

Hören 6A

1 – Trinkst du gern Kaffee?
– Nein danke.
2 – Ißt du gern Wurst?
– Oh ja, Wurst ist lecker.
3 – Möchtest du ein Ei?
– Ja, bitte.
4 – Ißt du gern Honig?
– Ugh! Nein, danke!
5 – Trinkst du gern Saft?
– Ja, bitte.
6 – Ißt du gern Käse?
– Ja, bitte!

Hören 6B

1 Halb zwei schon. Das Hähnchen wird kalt. Setz dich schnell hin. Möchtest du Pommes frites?
2 Hee, komm. Steh' auf! Der Kaffee ist auf dem Tisch. Möchtest du Müsli oder ein Ei heute?
3 – Noch eine Scheibe Schinken, Christof?
– Nein, danke. Ich habe schon Verspätung! Der Film beginnt um halb acht!

– Du hast noch Zeit. Iß noch ein Käsebrot.
4 – Ißt du lieber Marmelade oder Honig?
– Honig, bitte.
– Mit Toast, Brot oder Brötchen?
– Brötchen bitte.
– Und was trinkst du gern?
– Tee mit Milch, bitte.
5 – So, wir essen schnell vor der Sportschau. Es gibt Fußball um Viertel nach sieben heute abend.
– Möchtest du also Wurst oder Käse?
– Wurst, bitte – mit einer Scheibe Brot und einem Glas Cola.
6 – Also David, ißt du gern Frikadellen mit Pommes frites?
– Oh ja! Das ist lecker!
– Möchtest du auch Salat?
– Ja, bitte.
– So, was macht ihr zwei heute nachmittag?
– Oh, wir gehen in die Stadt. Es gibt einen guten Film im Kino um Viertel nach zwei.

Hören 6C

1 – Nicole, was trinkst du gern zum Frühstück?
– Oh, Kaffee oder Orangensaft.
– Möchtest du ein Ei?
– Ugh, nein! Ekelhaft! Ich hasse Eier!
2 – Lukas, was ißt du gern?
– Brötchen mit Marmelade.
– Und was trinkst du gern?
– Apfelsaft. Ich trinke aber nicht gern Kaffee.
3 – Petra, trinkst du gern Tee?
– Ja, ich trinke gerne Tee.
– Und was ißt du gern?
– Ein Ei, bitte.
4 – Carmen, was ißt du gern zum Frühstück?
– Brötchen mit Käse, bitte.
– Mit Käse?
– Ja, ich esse nicht gern Marmelade.
5 – Bruno, was trinkst du zum Frühstück?
– Oh, ich trinke gern Tee oder Kaffee.
– Möchtest du auch Orangensaft?
– Nein, danke. Ich trinke nicht gern Orangensaft.
6 – Karl, was ißt du gern zum Frühstück?
– Ich esse gern Brötchen mit Marmelade.
– Und was ißt du nicht gern?
– Käse!

Hören 6D

1 – Ja, Frau Wolf, wissen Sie, mein Sohn Johannes ist Vegetarier; er ißt nur Käse und Eier.
– Was? Nur Käse und Eier?
– Nein, nein! Natürlich nicht nur Käse und Eier, aber er ißt kein Fleisch, also keine Wurst, kein Hähnchen usw.
2 – Also Katja, was ißt du gern?
– Eigentlich fast alles: Brot, Käse, Salate, Hähnchen, Pommes natürlich ...
– Pommes frites? Aber sie sind so ungesund!
– Ja, ich weiß, sie schmecken aber gut!
– Und was trinkst du gern?
– Tja ... Limonade oder Cola.
– Aber sie sind doch so süß!
– Ja, ich weiß. Ich trinke auch gern Orangensaft, aber Limonade und Cola schmecken mir besser!

Sprechen 6A

1 Orangensaft
2 Wurst
3 Brötchen
4 Marmelade
5 Honig
6 Milch
7 Butter
8 Käse
9 Tee
10 Kaffee

Sprechen 6B

1 **A:** Was ißt und trinkst du zum Frühstück?
B: Ich esse Brötchen und Marmelade, und ich trinke Kaffee und Apfelsaft.
2 **A:** Was ißt und trinkst du zum Mittagessen?
B: Ich esse Hähnchen, Pommes frites und Salat, und ich trinke Cola.
3 **A:** Was ißt und trinkst du zum Abendessen?
B: Ich esse Brot, Schinken und Käse, und ich trinke Milch.
4 **A:** Was ißt und trinkst du zum Abendessen?
B: Ich esse Wurst, Brötchen und Eier, und ich trinke Limonade.
5 **A:** Was ißt und trinkst du zum Mittagessen?
B: Ich esse Salat, Frikadellen und Nudeln, und ich trinke Limonade.
6 **A:** Was ißt und trinkst du zum Frühstück?
B: Ich esse Toast mit Honig, und ich trinke Tee und Orangensaft.

Sprechen 6C

1 **A:** Was ißt du gern?
B: Ich esse gern Pommes frites.
A: Was trinkst du gern?
B: Ich trinke gern Orangensaft.
A: Was ißt du nicht gern?
B: Ich esse nicht gern Eier.
A: Was trinkst du nicht gern?
B: Ich trinke nicht gern Tee.
2 **A:** Was ißt du gerne?
B: Ich esse gern Käse.
A: Was trinkst du gern?
B: Ich trinke gern Kaffee.
A: Was ißt du nicht gerne?
B: Ich esse nicht gerne Wurst.
A: Was trinkst du nicht gerne?
B: Ich trinke nicht gern Milch.
3 **A:** Was ißt du gern?
B: Ich esse gern Brötchen.
A: Was trinkst du gern?
B: Ich trinke gerne Kakao.
A: Was ißt du nicht gerne?
B: Ich esse nicht gerne Honig.
A: Was trinkst du nicht gern?
B: Ich trinke nicht gerne Apfelsaft.

4 **A:** Was ißt du gerne?
B: Ich esse gerne Schinken.
A: Was trinkst du gerne?
B: Ich trinke gerne Cola.
A: Was ißt du nicht gerne?
B: Ich esse nicht gerne Brot.
A: Was trinkst du nicht gerne?
B: Ich trinke nicht gerne Limonade.

5 **A:** Was ißt du gern?
B: Ich esse gerne Frikadellen.
A: Was trinkst du gern?
B: Ich trinke gern Milch.
A: Was ißt du nicht gerne?
B: Ich esse nicht gerne Marmelade.
A: Was trinkst du nicht gern?
B: Ich trinke nicht gerne Kaffee.

6 **A:** Was ißt du gerne?
B: Ich esse gerne Hähnchen.
A: Was trinkst du gern?
B: Ich trinke gern Apfelsaft.
A: Was ißt du nicht gerne?
B: Ich esse nicht gerne Salat.
A: Was trinkst du nicht gern?
B: Ich trinke nicht gern Orangensaft.

Sprechen 6D

Beispiel
Zum Frühstück esse ich gern Müsli.
Ich trinke gern Kaffee.
Ich esse nicht gern Toast.
Ich trinke nicht gern Tee.
Zum Mittagessen esse ich gern Pommes frites.
Ich trinke gern Cola.
Ich esse nicht gern Wurst.
Ich trinke nicht gern Apfelsaft.
Zum Abendessen esse ich gern Käse.
Ich trinke gern Milch.
Ich esse nicht gern Schinken.
Ich trinke nicht gern Orangensaft.

7 Schule

Hören 7A

1 Mein Lieblingsfach ist Deutsch.
2 Mein Lieblingsfach ist Kunst.
3 Mein Lieblingsfach ist Physik.
4 Mein Lieblingsfach ist Geschichte.
5 Mein Lieblingsfach ist Französisch.
6 Mein Lieblingsfach ist Mathe.
7 Mein Lieblingsfach ist Werken.
8 Mein Lieblingsfach ist Englisch.
9 Mein Lieblingsfach ist Technik.

Hören 7B

1 – Wann machst du deine Schulaufgaben?
– Also, nach dem Mittagessen – normalerweise zwischen zwei und vier Uhr.

2 – Wann machst du deine Hausaufgaben?
– Vor dem Abendessen – zwischen Viertel nach fünf und Viertel nach sechs.

3 – Machst du deine Schulaufgaben nachmittags oder abends?
– Normalerweise abends, zwischen Viertel nach sieben und Viertel vor neun.

4 – Wann machst du deine Schulaufgaben?
– Nachmittags zwischen drei und halb fünf.

5 – Wann machst du deine Hausaufgaben?
– Normalerweise wenn ich nach Hause komme, also zwischen halb drei und halb vier.

Hören 7C

1 – Wie gefällt dir Deutsch?
– Deutsch ist mein Lieblingsfach – es ist interessant und gefällt mir sehr gut.

2 – Was lernst du nicht so gern?
– Mathe – es ist sehr langweilig!

3 – Welches Fach gefällt dir, Yusuf?
– Kunst. Ich male und zeichne sehr gern.

4 – Welches Fach gefällt dir nicht?
– Geschichte. Das interessiert mich nicht so sehr!

5 – Wie findest du Erdkunde?
– Na ja, es geht. Manchmal ist es interessant, und manchmal ist es langweilig.

6 – Gefällt dir Sport, Elke?
– Ja, natürlich! Es ist mein Lieblingsfach. Ich spiele gern Tennis und Volleyball.

7 – Wie gefällt dir Chemie?
– Der Lehrer ist ziemlich streng, aber es geht.

8 – Wie gefällt dir Englisch, Adam?
– Überhaupt nicht! Es ist stinklangweilig!

Sprechen 7A

1 Biologie
2 Deutsch
3 Musik
4 Mathe
5 Kunst
6 Chemie
7 Englisch
8 Geschichte
9 Erdkunde

Sprechen 7B

1 Englisch, Spanisch und Französisch
2 Biologie und Chemie
3 Physik, Musik, Mathematik
4 Maria Richter lernt Geschichte.

Sprechen 7C

Beispiele
1 Englisch gefällt mir – es ist interessant.
2 Deutsch ist ganz interessant.
3 Mein Lieblingsfach ist Kunst – es ist toll.
4 Sport gefällt mir – ich spiele gern Fußball.
5 Latein gefällt mir nicht – es ist langweilig!

Sprechen 7D

Beispiel
A: Was hast du in der ersten Stunde?
B: Erdkunde.
A: Wie findest du Erdkunde?
B: Es ist toll!

B: Was hast du in der zweiten Stunde?
A: Mathe.
B: Wie findest du Mathe?
A: Es ist langweilig.

8 Meine Freizeit

Hören 8A

1 Ich heiße Irene. Ich höre gern Musik.
2 Ich heiße Murat. Ich spiele Fußball.
3 Ich heiße Nicole. Ich lese gern.
4 Ich heiße Daniel. Ich reite.
5 Ich heiße Karl. Ich sehe fern.
6 Ich heiße Miriam. Ich spiele Klavier.

Hören 8B

1 Es ist sechzehn Uhr fünf.
2 Es ist dreiundzwanzig Uhr fünfzehn.
3 Es ist achtzehn Uhr dreißig.
4 Es ist zweiundzwanzig Uhr zehn.
5 Es ist einundzwanzig Uhr fünfundvierzig.
6 Es ist neunzehn Uhr fünfunddreißig.

Hören 8C

1 Komm schnell! *Lindenstraße* beginnt um achtzehn Uhr zehn!
2 – Wann beginnt *Sport aus aller Welt?*
– Um fünfzehn Uhr dreißig.
3 Ich will *Die Tiger von Kanha* um einundzwanzig Uhr fünf sehen.
4 – Wann ist *Guten Appetit*?
– Um dreizehn Uhr fünfundvierzig.
5 Ich sehe gern *Eurocops* um siebzehn Uhr fünfundfünfzig.
6 Ich will *Nachbarn* um vierzehn Uhr fünfundvierzig sehen.

Hören 8D

1 **Interviewer:** Was machst du am liebsten in deiner Freizeit, Anna?
Anna: Ich lese sehr gern, und zweimal im Monat gehe ich in die Disco.
2 **Interviewer:** Gehst du gern in die Disco, Jörg?
Jörg: Nein! Ich tanze nicht gern! Am liebsten fahre ich rad, oder ich bummle in der Stadt.
3 **Interviewer:** Was machst du am liebsten in deiner Freizeit, Tamara?
Tamara: Abends sehe ich normalerweise fern, aber am Wochenende gehe ich mit dem Hund spazieren.
4 **Interviewer:** Und du, Heike, was machst du?
Heike: Am liebsten fahre ich rad mit meiner Schwester und unseren Freunden.
5 **Interviewer:** Was machst du nach der Schule, Marek?
Marek: Ich bummle in der Stadt oder ich lese.
6 **Interviewer:** Liest du gern, Gerd?
Gerd: Nein! Das ist zu langweilig! Ich gehe lieber in die Disco.
7 **Interviewer:** Beate, was machst du?
Beate: Ich gehe mit dem Hund spazieren, und abends nach meinen Hausaufgaben sehe ich fern.
8 **Interviewer:** Was machst du am liebsten in deiner Freizeit, Sven?
Sven: Ich fahre rad und gehe oft mit meinem Hund spazieren.

Sprechen 8A

1 Ich spiele Fußball.
2 Ich spiele Tennis.
3 Ich sehe fern.
4 Ich gehe mit dem Hund spazieren.
5 Ich gehe in die Disco.
6 Ich schwimme.
7 Ich lese.
8 Ich reite.

Sprechen 8B

Beispiele
1 **A:** Wie findest du Musiksendungen?
B: Toll!
2 **A:** Wie findest du Trickfilme?
B: Doof!
3 **A:** Wie findest du Sportsendungen?
B: Interessant!
4 **A:** Wie findest du Natursendungen?
B: Super!
5 **A:** Wie findest du die Nachrichten?
B: Langweilig!
6 **A:** Wie findest du Filme?
B: Toll!

Sprechen 8C

Beispiel
Ich spiele gern Fußball in meiner Freizeit. Ich lese gern, ich spiele mit dem Computer, und ich höre gern Musik.
Am liebsten fahre ich rad, oder ich bummle in der Stadt.
Ich sehe ungefähr zehn Stunden pro Woche fern. Am liebsten sehe ich Filme und Serien. Ich sehe nicht gern Nachrichten – sie sind langweilig! Talkshows sind auch doof, aber Musiksendungen und Natursendungen sind interessant.

9 Was kostet das?

Hören 9A

1 – Was kostet ein Hamburger, bitte?
– 4,90 DM.
2 – Was kostet eine Bratwurst, bitte?
– 3,10 DM.
3 – Was kostet eine Frikadelle, bitte?
– 2,80 DM.
4 – Was kostet eine Portion Pommes frites?
– 1,90 DM.

5 – Was kostet ein Eis, bitte?
– 2,00 DM.

Hören 9B

1 – Einmal Bratwurst und eine Limo, bitte.
– So, das macht 5,10 DM.
2 – Eine Portion Pommes und eine Limonade, bitte.
– 3,90 DM, bitte.
3 – Zweimal Schaschlik und ein Glas Orangensaft.
– Bitte schön. Das macht 10,00 DM.
4 – Einmal Vanilleeis und zweimal Cola, bitte.
– Also 5,00 DM, bitte.
5 – Einmal Hamburger und Pommes, bitte.
– Möchtest du auch etwas zu trinken?
– Ja, einen Apfelsaft, bitte.
– So, 8,80 DM, bitte.
6 – Dreimal Erdbeereis und zweimal Limonade, bitte.
– 7,00 DM, bitte.

Hören 9C

1 – Kommst du mit zum Jahrmarkt?
– Nein, ich spare mein Geld für Kleider und einen neuen Computer.
2 – Wofür sparst du dein Geld?
– Also, im Moment spare ich für mein Hobby; ich spiele jeden Mittwoch Tennis.
3 – Sparst du dein Geld, oder gibst du es aus?
– Ich gebe mein Geld aus! Ich kaufe mir CDs, Zeitschriften und Bücher, Bonbons und Snacks.
4 – Wofür gibst du dein Geld aus?
– Meistens für Kleider.
5 – Und du, Bianca, was machst du mit deinem Geld?
– Ich spare mein Geld für ein neues Rad.
6 – Wofür sparst du dein Geld, Michael?
– Für Kassetten für meinen Bruder: er hat im Juni Geburtstag.
7 – Was machst du mit deinem Geld?
– Ich gebe es für Kleider, Bücher usw. aus.
8 – Sparst du dein Geld, oder gibst du es aus?
– Im Moment spare ich für den Jahrmarkt im Oktober.

Sprechen 9A

1 Eine Mark und eine Mark neunundneunzig. Das macht zwei Mark neunundneunzig.
2 Vier Mark fünf und neunundneunzig Pfennig. Das macht fünf Mark und vier Pfennig.
3 Acht Mark zehn und drei Mark zwanzig. Das macht elf Mark dreißig.
4 Zweiundsiebzig Mark fünfzig und neun Mark fünfzehn. Das macht einundachtzig Mark fünfundsechzig.

Sprechen 9B

1 Ich möchte ein Zitroneneis, bitte.
2 Einmal Bratwurst und zwei Frikadellen, bitte.
3 Was macht das, bitte?
4 Ich spare für Turnschuhe.
5 Ich fahre mit Renates Riesenrad.

Sprechen 9C

Beispiele
1 Was kostet das?
2 Was nimmst du?
3 Wofür sparst du?
4 Wofür gibst du dein Geld aus?
5 Fährst du gern mit der Achterbahn?

Sprechen 9D

1 – Was nimmst du, Martin?
– Eine Cola und Pommes frites, bitte.
– Und ich nehme eine Bratwurst, eine Portion Pommes und eine Cola. Also, eine Bratwurst, zwei Portionen Pommes und zweimal Cola, bitte.
2 – Was nimmst du, Hella?
– Ein Eis und einen Apfelsaft, bitte.
– Und ich nehme ein Eis und eine Cola. Also, zweimal Eis, einen Apfelsaft und eine Cola, bitte.
3 – Was nimmst du, Friedrich?
– Eine Frikadelle, eine Portion Pommes und eine Limonade, bitte.
– Und ich nehme ein Schaschlik und Pommes. Also, eine Frikadelle, ein Schaschlik, zwei Portionen Pommes frites und eine Limonade, bitte.
4 – Was nimmst du, Dagmar?
– Einen Hamburger und eine Limo, bitte.
– Und ich nehme eine Wurst, ein Eis und einen Apfelsaft. Also einen Hamburger, eine Limo, eine Wurst, ein Eis und einen Apfelsaft.
5 – Was nimmst du, Hasan?
– Zweimal Eis und eine Cola, bitte.
– Und ich nehme eine Packung Chips und eine Cola. Also, zwei Eis, zweimal Cola und eine Packung Chips.
6 – Was nimmst du, Tara?
– Ein Butterbrot mit Käse und ein Schaschlik, bitte.
– Und ich nehme einen Hamburger und eine Packung Chips. Also, ein Butterbrot mit Käse, ein Schaschlik, einen Hamburger, und eine Packung Chips.

10 Wie schön!

Hören 10A

Berlin: Die Sonne scheint.
London: Es ist sehr kalt.
Paris: Es ist windig.
Rom: Es schneit.
Lissabon: Es regnet.
Warschau: Es ist neblig.
Athen: Es ist sehr heiß.

Hören 10B

1 Der Schultag ist länger in Großbritannien.
2 Fast jede Familie in Großbritannien hat ein Haustier.
3 In Deutschland essen wir mehr Brot als in Großbritannien.
4 Ich glaube, daß die meisten Engländer ein Haus mit Garten haben.

5 Ich glaube, daß die Kinder in Deutschland mehr Freizeit am Nachmittag für ihre Hobbys haben.
6 Ich finde die Werbung und Fernsehsendungen in Großbritannien interessanter als in Deutschland.

Hören 10C

1 **Interviewer:** Was machst du im Sommer, Barbara?
Barbara: Ich fahre ans Meer. Wir wohnen zwei Wochen in einem Hotel in Spanien.
2 **Interviewer:** Fährst du im Sommer weg, Ines?
Ines: Ja, ich fahre mit meinen Freunden aufs Land. Wir wohnen in einer Jugendherberge in der Nähe von Heidelberg.
3 **Interviewer:** Wohin fährst du, Stefan?
Stefan: Ich fahre mit meiner Familie ins Gebirge. Wir wohnen in einem Hotel und gehen jeden Tag wandern.
4 **Interviewer:** Was machst du im Sommer, Joachim?
Joachim: Ich fahre nach Irland. Meine Jugendgruppe bleibt zwei Wochen da. Wir wohnen in Zelten auf dem Lande.
5 **Interviewer:** Fährst du dieses Jahr wieder nach Spanien, Elisabeth?
Elisabeth: Nein, wir fahren erst im Winter weg. Ich verbringe Weihnachten in einem Ferienhaus im Gebirge.
6 **Interviewer:** Was machst du im Sommer, Hermann?
Hermann: Ich fahre mit meiner Familie nach Frankreich.
Interviewer: Wohnst du in einem Ferienhaus?
Hermann: Nein, in einem Zelt am Meer.

Hören 10D

Mutter: Krämer.
Ute: Hallo Mutti!
M: Ute! Wie geht's?
U: Super! Das Dorf liegt mitten im Gebirge, und das Ferienhaus ist schön und bequem.
M: Habt ihr viel Schnee?
U: Ja, es schneit im Moment, aber tagsüber ist das Wetter wunderschön, und die Sonne scheint.
M: Und was machst du?
U: Jeden Tag fahren wir ski – von halb zehn bis ungefähr halb fünf. Es ist toll!
M: Machst du viel abends?
U: Nein – ich bin zu müde! Meistens lese ich, oder ich sehe fern, aber am letzten Abend gibt es eine Disco. Also, mein Geld ist alle ... bis bald! Tschüs!

Sprechen 10A

1 Die Sonne scheint.
2 Es regnet.
3 Es ist windig.
4 Es ist neblig.
5 Es ist heiß.
6 Es ist kalt.
7 Es schneit.

Sprechen 10B

1 **A:** Was machst du im Sommer?
B: Ich fahre aufs Land. Ich wohne in einem Zelt.
2 **A:** Was machst du im Sommer?
B: Ich fahre ins Gebirge. Ich wohne in einer Jugendherberge.
3 **A:** Was machst du im Sommer?
B: Ich fahre an die See. Ich wohne in einem Hotel.
4 **A:** Was machst du im Sommer?
B: Ich fahre nicht weg. Ich bleibe zu Hause.
5 **A:** Was machst du im Sommer?
B: Ich fahre ins Gebirge. Ich wohne in einem Ferienhaus.
6 **A:** Was machst du im Sommer?
B: Ich fahre ans Meer. Ich wohne in einem Zelt.

Sprechen 10C

1 **B:** Wohin fährst du?
A: Ich fahre aufs Land.
B: Mit wem fährst du?
A: Ich fahre mit meiner Familie.
B: Wie lange bleibst du?
A: Zwei Wochen.
B: Was machst du?
A: Ich fahre rad, ich lese und ich sehe fern.
2 **A:** Wohin fährst du?
B: Ich fahre an die See.
A: Mit wem fährst du?
B: Ich fahre alleine.
A: Wie lange bleibst du?
B: Eine Woche.
A: Was machst du?
B: Ich schwimme, ich spiele Tennis, und ich gehe in die Disco.

Sprechen 10D

Ich fahre am liebsten nach Frankreich. Ich fahre mit meiner Familie ans Meer. Wir wohnen dort zwei Wochen in einem Ferienhaus. Das Wetter ist sehr schön – die Sonne scheint, und es ist sehr warm.

Ich schwimme, ich fahre rad, und ich spiele Fußball und Tennis. Ich bummle auch in der Stadt. Abends lese ich, oder ich sehe fern.

Abschlußtest (Kapitel 1–10)

Hören 1–10A

1 Guten Morgen!
2 Seite fünfundzwanzig, bitte!
3 Packt eure Sachen weg.
4 Hört gut zu!
5 Setzt euch!
6 Schreibt das in euer Heft.

Hören 1–10B

– Neunundzwanzig ... vierundfünfzig ... zwölf ... achtundsechzig ... fünfundvierzig ... dreißig ... sechsundachtzig ... zweiundneunzig ... siebenundvierzig ... dreizehn ... einundzwanzig ... vierundsiebzig ...
– Bingo!

Hören 1–10C

1 Ich heiße Dieter. Ich wohne in einem Einfamilienhaus in der Stadtmitte.

2 Ich heiße Susi. Ich habe ein Pferd und zwei Katzen.
3 Mein Name ist Alexandra. Ich habe einen Bruder und eine jüngere Stiefschwester.
4 Mein Name ist Yusuf. Ich spiele gern Fußball, und ich höre gern Musik.
5 Ich heiße Nicole. Ich komme aus Österreich. Ich wohne in einem Dorf in der Nähe von Salzburg.

Hören 1–10D

1 Ich wohne in einem Reihenhaus am Stadtrand.
2 Ich lerne gern Kunst und Erdkunde. Werken gefällt mir nicht.
3 Ich stehe um halb sieben auf.
4 Ich fahre ins Gebirge und wohne in einem Ferienhaus.
5 Ich trinke gern Kaffee, und ich esse gern Brötchen. Ich esse nicht gern Wurst.
6 Um halb acht gehe ich ins Kino.

Hören 1–10E

1 – Wie ist das Wetter in Österreich?
– Schlecht! Und in Deutschland?
2 – Was ist dein Lieblingsfach?
– Geschichte. Was lernst du am liebsten?
3 – Was machst du im Sommer?
– Ich fahre aufs Land. Und du?
4 – Was machst du in deiner Freizeit?
– Am liebsten spiele ich Fußball. Und du?
5 – Was ißt du gern?
– Pommes frites. Was ißt du gern?
6 – Wofür gibst du dein Geld aus?
– Für Kleider. Und du?

Hören 1–10F

Ich heiße Hans-Dieter Meier. Man schreibt Meier M-E-I-E-R. Ich bin vierzehn Jahre alt, und mein Geburtstag ist am 17. Juli. Meine Adresse ist Mozartweg 54, Ulm, und meine Telefonnummer ist 94 32 86.

Sprechen 1–10A

1 Ein Kuli
2 Cola
3 Geld
4 Ein Lineal
5 Ein Heft
6 Schokolade
7 Kassetten
8 Turnschuhe
9 Ein Buch

Sprechen 1–10B

1 Dirk: D-I-R-K
2 Pawel: P-A-W-E-L
3 Josefa: J-O-S-E-F-A
4 Micha: M-I-C-H-A
5 Birgit: B-I-R-G-I-T
6 Vera: V-E-R-A

Sprechen 1–10C

A: Wie heißt du?
B: Ich heiße Kirsten Pfeifer. Und du?
A: Ich heiße Peter Müller.
B: Wie alt bist du?
A: Ich bin dreizehn Jahre alt. Wie alt bist du?
B: Ich bin zwölf.
A: Wo wohnst du?
B: Ich wohne in Schwerin. Wo wohnst du?
A: In Mannheim.
B: Hast du Geschwister?
A: Ja, ich habe einen Bruder. Hast du Geschwister?
B: Ja, ich habe eine Schwester.

Sprechen 1–10D

Beispiel
A: Wie heißt du?
B: Ich heiße Samuela.
A: Hast du Geschwister?
B: Ja, ich habe zwei Brüder und eine Schwester.
A: Hast du Haustiere?
B: Ich habe einen Hund.
A: Was ißt du gern?
B: Ich esse gern Schaschlik und Pommes.
A: Was ist dein Lieblingsfach?
B: Chemie. Das ist interessant.
A: Was machst du am liebsten in deiner Freizeit?
B: Ich lese, und ich schwimme.
A: Wofür gibst du dein Geld aus?
B: Ich gebe mein Geld für Bücher aus.
A: Wohin fährst du im Sommer?
B: Ich fahre mit meiner Familie ans Meer.

Sprechen 1–10E

4 Mein Stundenplan und Hausaufgaben (Montags)
Am Montag in der ersten Stunde habe ich Geschichte. Das geht. In der zweiten und dritten Stunden habe ich Sport. Das ist toll! Sport ist mein Lieblingsfach. In der vierten Stunde habe ich Deutsch. Das gefällt mir, aber in der fünften Stunde habe ich Erdkunde. Das gefällt mir nicht – es ist langweilig!
Ich mache meine Hausaufgaben zwischen fünf und halb sieben. Montag mache ich Geschichte, Deutsch und Erdkunde.

1 Hallo! Wie heißt du?

Hören 1A

1 Thomas
2 Melanie
3 Tamara
4 Christof
5 Karl-Heinz
6 Anneli

NATIONAL CURRICULUM LEVEL 1 Total: 6 points
(and AT3 Level 1 and AT4 Level 1)

Hören 1B

1 K **2** h,i,e **3** y,a **4** r,j,o **5** W,z,v

NATIONAL CURRICULUM LEVEL 1 Total: 12 points

Hören 1C

Guido 3
Sonja 10
Elke 0
Peter 7
Uwe 8
Katrin 5

NATIONAL CURRICULUM LEVEL 1 Total: 6 points

Hören 1D

Heidi 11
Stefan 14
Ute 12
Joachim 7
Christiane 15
Adam 10

NATIONAL CURRICULUM LEVEL 2 Total: 6 points

Sprechen 1A

1 das Heft
2 der Tisch
3 der Stuhl
4 der Kuli
5 die Mappe
6 die Tür

NATIONAL CURRICULUM LEVEL 1 Total: 6 points

Sprechen 1B

Journalistin: Guten Tag.
Du: Guten Tag.
Journalistin: Wie heißt du?
Du: Ich heiße *(name)*.
Journalistin: Wie schreibt man das?
Du: *(Spell name)*
Journalistin: Wie alt bist du?
Du: Ich bin *(age)* (Jahre alt).

NATIONAL CURRICULUM LEVEL 2 Total: 4 points
(and AT1 Level 2)

Sprechen 1C

Beispiel
Maria/Karl: Wie heißt du?
Achim/Gabi: Ich heiße Achim/Gabi. Und du?/Wie heißt du?
M/K: Ich heiße Maria/Karl.
A/G: Wie alt bist du?
M/K: Ich bin elf (Jahre alt). Wie alt bist du?
A/G: Ich bin zwölf (Jahre alt).

NATIONAL CURRICULUM LEVEL 2
Total: 4 points each

Lesen 1A

A4, B1, C6, D2, E5, F3

NATIONAL CURRICULUM LEVEL 1 Total: 6 points

Lesen 1B

1C, 2H, 3J, 4B, 5D, 6A, 7I, 8G, 9E, 10F

NATIONAL CURRICULUM LEVEL 2 Total: 10 points

Lesen 1C

A3, B6, C4, D1, E5, F2

NATIONAL CURRICULUM LEVEL 2 Total: 6 points

Lesen 1D

1 BARBARA 10
2 OLIVER 11
3 GRETE 13
4 FLORIAN 9

NATIONAL CURRICULUM LEVEL 2 Total: 8 points
(and AT4 Level 1)

Lesen 1E

1 Hallo, Vater. Tag, Renate.
2 Ich heiße Kai. Ich bin drei.
3 Moment Ulli! Hier ist ein Kuli.
4 Hör gut zu: Wie heißt du?
5 Nummer eins ist Karl-Heinz.
6 Ich bin Piet. Ich singe ein Lied.

NATIONAL CURRICULUM LEVEL 2 Total: 6 points

Schreiben 1A

1 drei
2 zwölf
3 der Kuli
4 der Tisch
5 das Heft
6 Grüß dich!

NATIONAL CURRICULUM LEVEL 1 Total: 6 points

Schreiben 1B

(Sentences paired as follows:)
Guten Tag!
Guten Tag!

Wie heißt du?
Ich heiße Sven.

Wie alt bist du?
Ich bin zwölf Jahre alt.
(3rd pair of sentences could precede 2nd pair.)

NATIONAL CURRICULUM LEVEL 2 (and AT3 Level 2) Total: 6 points

Schreiben 1C

1 elf
2 Stuhl
3 Tür
4 Mappe/Tasche
5 acht
6 heiße/bin

NATIONAL CURRICULUM LEVEL 2 Total: 6 points

2 *Wo wohnst du?*

Hören 2A

See table below.

NATIONAL CURRICULUM LEVEL 1 (and AT3 Level 1) Total: 6 points

Hören 2B

Tobias – Stuttgart
Bärbel – Hamburg
Peter – Wien
Monika – Schwerin
Christel – Salzburg
Hans – Hannover

NATIONAL CURRICULUM LEVEL 2 (and AT3 Level 1) Total: 6 points

Hören 2C

im Norden: 4, 8
in Westen: 1, 5
im Osten: 2, 7
im Süden: 3, 6

NATIONAL CURRICULUM LEVEL 2 (and AT3 Level 1) Total: 8 points

Sprechen 2A

1 Ich komme aus England.
2 Ich komme aus Frankreich.
3 Ich komme aus Deutschland.
4 Ich komme aus Dänemark.
5 Ich komme aus Schottland.
6 Ich komme aus Irland.
7 Ich komme aus Wales.
8 Ich komme aus Italien.

NATIONAL CURRICULUM LEVEL 1 Total: 8 points

Sprechen 2B

1 Ich heiße Erik. Ich komme aus Deutschland. Ich wohne in Hamburg. Das liegt im Norden.
2 Ich heiße Uschi. Ich komme aus Deutschland. Ich wohne in Berlin. Das liegt im Osten.
3 Ich heiße Lars. Ich komme aus Österreich. Ich wohne in Wien. Das liegt im Norden.
4 Ich heiße Kai. Ich komme aus Deutschland. Ich wohne in München. Das liegt im Süden.
5 Ich heiße Susi. Ich komme aus der Schweiz. Ich wohne in Zürich. Das liegt im Norden.
6 Ich heiße Ute. Ich komme aus Deutschland. Ich wohne in Köln. Das liegt im Westen.

NATIONAL CURRICULUM LEVEL 2 (and AT3 Level 1) Total: 8 points

Sprechen 2C

1 Ich heiße *(name)*.
2 Ich komme aus *(country)*.
3 Ich wohne in *(city/town/village)*.
4 Das liegt im *(compass point)*.

NATIONAL CURRICULUM LEVEL 2 (and AT3 Level 2) Total: 4 points

Lesen 2A

1F, 2D, 3A, 4E, 5C, 6B

NATIONAL CURRICULUM LEVEL 1 Total: 6 points

Lesen 2B

1A, 2D, 3F, 4B, 5E, 6C

NATIONAL CURRICULUM LEVEL 2 Total: 6 points

Lesen 2C

A5, B3, C1, D6, E2, F4

NATIONAL CURRICULUM LEVEL 2 Total: 6 points

Lesen 2D

1D, 2A, 3E, 4B, 5F, 6C

NATIONAL CURRICULUM LEVEL 2 Total: 6 points

Schreiben 2A

B = Belgien
A = Österreich
F = Frankreich
D = Deutschland
DK = Dänemark
I = Italien

NATIONAL CURRICULUM LEVEL 1 (and AT3 Level 1) Total: 6 points

	Deutschland	Österreich	Schweiz	Frankreich	Belgien	Dänemark
Anja	✔					
Axel			✔			
Elisabeth						✔
Yannick				✔		
Marie					✔	
Thorsten		✔				

Schreiben 2B

1 Wie heißt du?
2 Woher kommst du?
3 Wo wohnst du?
4 Wo liegt das?

NATIONAL CURRICULUM LEVEL 2 (and AT3 Level 2) Total: 4 points

Schreiben 2C

1 Wo woh*nst* du?
2 Ich w*ohne* in Birmingham.
3 Hallo! Ich ko*mme* aus Belgien.
4 Frankfurt ist in D*eutsch*land.
5 Newport ist in der *Nähe* von Dundee.
6 Hamburg ist im No*rden*.

NATIONAL CURRICULUM LEVEL 2 (and AT3 Level 2) Total: 6 points

3 Meine Familie

Hören 3A

Steffi – fish
Britta – horse
Michael – dog
Lars – cat
Julia – mouse
Niko – rabbit

NATIONAL CURRICULUM LEVEL 1 Total: 6 points

Hören 3B

1 ✔ **2** ✗ **3** ✔ **4** ✗ **5** ✔ **6** ✗

NATIONAL CURRICULUM LEVEL 2 Total: 6 points

Hören 3C

See table below.

NATIONAL CURRICULUM LEVEL 2 (and AT3 Level 1) Total: 9 points

Sprechen 3A

1 A: Was ist das?
B: Das ist ein Hund.
2 A: Was ist das?
B: Das ist eine Katze.
3 A: Was ist das?
B: Das ist eine Maus.
4 A: Was ist das?
B: Das ist ein Kaninchen.
5 A: Was ist das?
B: Das ist ein Pferd.
6 A: Was ist das?
B: Das ist ein Meerschweinchen.

NATIONAL CURRICULUM LEVEL 1 Total: 6 points

Sprechen 3B

1 Ich heiße Paul. Ich habe eine Schwester.
2 Ich heiße Sabine. Ich habe einen Bruder.
3 Ich heiße Andreas. Ich habe eine Katze und einen Hund.
4 Ich heiße Marion. Ich habe zwei Brüder und ein Kaninchen.
5 Ich heiße Jutta. (Ich bin ein Einzelkind, und) ich habe ein Pferd.
6 Ich heiße Raphael. Ich habe zwei Schwestern und einen Hamster.

NATIONAL CURRICULUM LEVEL 2 Total: 6 points

Sprechen 3C

1 Wie heißt du?
2 Wo wohnst du?
3 Wie alt bist du?
4 Hast du Geschwister?
5 Hast du ein Haustier?

NATIONAL CURRICULUM LEVEL 2 (and AT3 Level 2) Total: 5 points

Sprechen 3D

– Wie heißt du?
– Ich heiße *(name)*.
– Wie alt bist du?
– Ich bin *(age)* (Jahre alt).
– Hast du Geschwister?
– Ich habe *(brothers/sisters)*./Nein. Ich bin Einzelkind.
– Hast du ein Haustier?
– Ja. Ich habe *(pet)*./Nein. Ich habe keine Haustiere.

NATIONAL CURRICULUM LEVELS 2,3 (and AT3 Level 2 and AT3 Level 1) Total: 8 points

Lesen 3A

1 die Katze
2 die Maus
3 das Pferd
4 der Hund
5 das Meerschweinchen
6 das Kaninchen

NATIONAL CURRICULUM LEVEL 1 Total: 6 points

	Einzelkind	1 Bruder	1 Schwester	2 Brüder	2 Schwestern	3 Brüder	3 Schwestern
Micha		✔	✔				
Elena					✔		
Nadine	✔						
Johann			✔	✔			
Jasmin		✔					✔
Richard		✔					

Lesen 3B

A3, B5, C2, D4, E6, F1

NATIONAL CURRICULUM LEVEL 2 Total: 6 points

Lesen 3C

1C, 2E, 3A, 4D, 5B

NATIONAL CURRICULUM LEVEL 2 Total: 5 points

Lesen 3D

1 richtig
2 falsch
3 richtig
4 falsch
5 falsch
6 richtig

NATIONAL CURRICULUM LEVEL 3 Total: 6 points
(and AT4 Level 1)

Schreiben 3A

1 der Fisch
2 die Katze
3 der Hund
4 das Pferd
5 das Kaninchen
6 das Meerschweinchen

NATIONAL CURRICULUM LEVEL 1 Total: 6 points

Schreiben 3B

1 Hast du Geschwister?
2 Ich habe zwei Schwestern.
3 Mein Bruder heißt Paul.
4 Ich habe keine Haustiere.
5 Wie alt ist deine Schwester?
6 Ich habe zwei Brüder und eine Schwester.

NATIONAL CURRICULUM LEVEL 2 Total: 6 points
(and AT3 Level 1)

Schreiben 3C

1 Ich habe einen *Hund*.
2 Ich heiße Dorit. Ich habe einen *Bruder* und eine *Schwester*.
3 Ich habe *drei Brüder* und eine *Maus*.

NATIONAL CURRICULUM LEVEL 2 Total: 6 points
(and AT3 Level 2)

4 Bei mir zu Hause

Hören 4A

Dieter 78
Sara 51
Nils 24
Nina 32
Josef 96
Heidi 45

NATIONAL CURRICULUM LEVEL 1 Total: 6 points

Hören 4B

1B, 2F, 3D, 4A, 5C, 6E

NATIONAL CURRICULUM LEVEL 1 Total: 6 points

Hören 4C

1C, 2D, 3A, 4E, 5F, 6B

NATIONAL CURRICULUM LEVEL 2 Total: 6 points

Hören 4D

1 Küche
2 Schlafzimmer
3 Toilette
4 Eßzimmer
5 Küche

NATIONAL CURRICULUM LEVEL 2, 3 Total: 5 points
(and AT3 Level 1)

Sprechen 4A

1 (Martina Becker:) ein Meter einundneunzig.
2 (Gabi Schwarz:) ein Meter dreiundsiebzig.
3 (Anna Heilmann:) ein Meter fünfundachtzig.
4 (Steffi Risch:) ein Meter achtundsechzig.
5 (Marion Jurek:) ein Meter siebenundachtzig.
6 (Sandra Palm:) ein Meter neunundvierzig.

NATIONAL CURRICULUM LEVEL 1 Total: 6 points

Sprechen 4B

Hier ist das Eßzimmer.
Hier ist die Küche.
Hier ist das Wohnzimmer.
Hier ist der Keller.
Hier ist mein Zimmer.
Hier ist das Schlafzimmer von meinen Eltern.
Hier ist das Badezimmer.
Hier ist die Toilette.

NATIONAL CURRICULUM LEVEL 2 Total: 8 points

Sprechen 4C

1 **A:** Wie heißt du?
B: Ich heiße Tanja Dennen.
A: Wie ist deine Adresse?
B: Meine Adresse ist Schulstraße 21.
A: Wie ist deine Telefonnummer?
B: Meine Telefonnummer ist 71 14 02.
2 **A:** Wie heißt du?
B: Ich heiße Tamara Englert.
A: Wie ist deine Adresse?
B: Meine Adresse ist Hauptstraße 12.
A: Wie ist deine Telefonnummer?
B: Meine Telefonnummer ist 62 11.
3 **A:** Wie heißt du?
B: Ich heiße Andreas Fischer.
A: Wie ist deine Adresse?
B: Meine Adresse ist Friedrichstraße 83.
A: Wie ist deine Telefonnummer?
B: Meine Telefonnummer ist 67 41 08.
4 **A:** Wie heißt du?
B: Ich heiße Paul Kempf.

A: Wie ist deine Adresse?
B: Meine Adresse ist Lindenstraße 36.
A: Wie ist deine Telefonnummer?
B: Meine Telefonnummer ist 47 22 66.

5 A: Wie heißt du?
B: Ich heiße Silke Tast.
A: Wie ist deine Adresse?
B: Meine Adresse ist Gartenstraße 52.
A: Wie ist deine Telefonnummer?
B: Meine Telefonnummer ist 15 85.

6 A: Wie heißt du?
B: Ich heiße Christian Werner.
A: Wie ist deine Adresse?
B: Meine Adresse ist Hermannstraße 28.
A: Wie ist deine Telefonnummer?
B: Meine Telefonnummer ist 91 28 35.

NATIONAL CURRICULUM LEVELS 2, 3
(and AT1 Level 2) Total: 3 points each per conversation
(and AT3 Level 2)

Sprechen 4D

1 A: Wo wohnst du?
B: Ich wohne in der Stadtmitte. Wir haben ein Haus.

2 A: Wo wohnst du?
B: Ich wohne in einem Dorf. Wir haben einen Bungalow.

3 A: Wo wohnst du?
B: Ich wohne in der Stadmitte. Wir haben eine Wohnung.

4 A: Wo wohnst du?
B: Ich wohne am Stadtrand. Wir haben ein Haus.

5 A: Wo wohnst du?
B: Ich wohne in der Stadtmitte. Wir haben ein Reihenhaus.

6 A: Wo wohnst du?
B: Ich wohne am Stadtrand. Wir haben eine Wohnung.

NATIONAL CURRICULUM LEVEL 2
Total: 2 points per conversation (B role only)

Lesen 4A

einundzwanzig – 21
sechsundzwanzig – 26
fünfunddreißig – 35
achtundvierzig – 48
vierundfünfzig – 54
siebenundsechzig – 67
dreiundsiebzig – 73
neunundachtzig – 89
zweiundneunzig – 92
hundert – 100

NATIONAL CURRICULUM LEVEL 1 Total: 10 points

Lesen 4B

1D, 2C, 3A, 4E, 5B

NATIONAL CURRICULUM LEVEL 2 Total: 5 points

Lesen 4C

Deutsch	**Englisch**
Bauernhaus	farmhouse
Hausfrau	housewife
Hausmeister	caretaker
Haustür	front door
Parkhaus	car park
Rathaus	Town Hall
Stadtplan	town plan
Stadtviertel	district

NATIONAL CURRICULUM LEVEL 2b Total: 8 points

Lesen 4D

1D, 2A, 3E, 4C, 5B

NATIONAL CURRICULUM LEVEL 3 Total: 5 points

Schreiben 4A

1 wohnst
2 Stadtmitte
3 Wohnung
4 haben
5 Adresse
6 Telefonnummer

NATIONAL CURRICULUM LEVEL 1 Total: 6 points
(and AT3 Level 2)

Schreiben 4B

1 Wo wohnst du?
2 Ich wohne in einem Dorf.
3 Wir haben ein Einfamilienhaus.
4 Es ist ganz alt.
5 Wir haben sechs Zimmer.
6 Meine Adresse ist Mozartweg 6.

NATIONAL CURRICULUM LEVEL 2 Total: 6 points
(and AT3 Level 2)

Schreiben 4C

1 eine Wohnung
2 ein Haus
3 das Eßzimmer
4 das Badezimmer
5 die Toilette
6 der Keller

NATIONAL CURRICULUM LEVEL 2 Total: 6 points

5 *Mein Alltag*

Hören 5A

(Clock faces should show the following times:)

1 2 o'clock
2 a quarter to 5
3 half past 6
4 ten past 9
5 twenty-five to 3
6 a quarter to 12
7 half past 9
8 five to 8
9 twenty past 4

NATIONAL CURRICULUM LEVEL 1 Total: 9 points

Hören 5B

Jens – 14.4.
Jutta – 4.10.
Markus – 22.3.
Alexander – 23.7.
Petra – 6.8.
Oliver – 19.2.
Brigitte – 16.9.
Nadine – 31.5.

NATIONAL CURRICULUM LEVEL 1 Total: 8 points

Hören 5C

Formel eins – 27.5. – 12:45
Guten Morgen – 28.5. – 7:30
Horoskop – 31.5. – 9:25
Yogi Bär – 1.6. – 9:55
Raumschiff Enterprise – 3.6. – 11:20
Sport extra – 17.6. – 12:15

NATIONAL CURRICULUM LEVEL 2 Total: 12 points

Hören 5D

See table below.

NATIONAL CURRICULUM LEVEL 2 Total: 10 points
(and AT3 Level 2)

Sprechen 5A

1 Es ist sieben Uhr.
2 Es ist Viertel nach drei.
3 Es ist zwanzig nach neun.
4 Es ist Viertel vor sieben.
5 Es ist fünfundzwanzig vor eins.
6 Es ist halb acht.
7 Es ist zehn vor vier.
8 Es ist fünf nach zwei.
9 Es ist halb zwölf.

NATIONAL CURRICULUM LEVEL 1 Total: 9 points

Sprechen 5B

Es ist Viertel vor zwei. Ich stehe auf.
Es ist Viertel nach drei. Ich sehe fern.
Es ist halb sechs. Ich esse.
Es ist fünfundzwanzig nach sieben. Ich verlasse das Haus.
Es ist acht Uhr. Ich treffe mich mit Freunden.
Es ist zehn nach vier. Ich gehe ins Bett.

NATIONAL CURRICULUM LEVEL 2
Total: 12 points (1 point per sentence)

Sprechen 5C

1 A: Wann hast du Geburtstag?
B: Ich habe am 14. März Geburtstag.
2 B: Wann hast du Geburtstag?
A: Ich habe am 24. Oktober Geburtstag.
3 A: Wann hast du Geburtstag?
B: Ich habe am 29. Juni Geburtstag.
4 B: Wann hast du Geburtstag?
A: Ich habe am 2. September Geburtstag.
5 A: Wann hast du Geburtstag?
B: Ich habe am 7. Januar Geburtstag.
6 B: Wann hast du Geburtstag?
A: Ich habe am 1. Mai Geburtstag.

NATIONAL CURRICULUM LEVEL 2
Total: 3 points each

Sprechen 5D

(About 6 sentences about daily routine, preferably combining activity and time:)
Beispiel
Ich stehe um Viertel vor sieben auf.
Ich wasche mich um zehn vor sieben.
Ich frühstücke um sieben Uhr.
Ich sehe um Viertel nach sieben fern.
Ich verlasse das Haus um halb acht.
Ich treffe mich mit meinen Freunden um fünf nach acht.
(*It is also acceptable to separate activities from times, e.g.* Es ist Viertel vor sieben. Ich stehe auf.)

NATIONAL CURRICULUM LEVEL 3 Total: 6 points

Lesen 5A

1F, 2C, 3B, 4E, 5A, 6D

NATIONAL CURRICULUM LEVEL 1 Total: 6 points

Lesen 5B

1D, 2F, 3B, 4C, 5E, 6A

NATIONAL CURRICULUM LEVEL 2 Total: 6 points

Lesen 5C

1 Ich sehe fern.
2 Ich treffe mich mit Freunden.
3 Ich wasche mich.
4 Ich frühstücke.
5 Ich gehe ins Bett.
6 Die Schule ist aus.

NATIONAL CURRICULUM LEVEL 2 Total: 6 points

	ich gehe in die Stadt	ich mache meine Hausaufgaben	ich treffe mich mit Freunden	ich esse	ich sehe fern	ich gehe ins Bett
Anna					✔	✔
Ralf		✔				
Kasimir			✔	✔		
Sabine	✔		✔			
Dorit						✔
Werner		✔			✔	

Lesen 5D

1 falsch
2 falsch
3 richtig
4 falsch
5 richtig

NATIONAL CURRICULUM LEVEL 3 (and AT4 Level 1) Total: 5 points

Schreiben 5A

1 Oktober
2 März
3 Januar
4 Dezember
5 Juni
6 Februar

NATIONAL CURRICULUM LEVEL 1 Total: 6 points

Schreiben 5B

(Sentences should be paired as follows:)
Wann hast du Geburtstag?
Ich habe am 21. Juli Geburtstag.

Wie alt bist du?
Ich bin dreizehn Jahre alt.

Was machst du?
Ich treffe mich mit Freunden.
(These pairs in any order are acceptable.)

NATIONAL CURRICULUM LEVEL 2 (and AT3 Level 2) Total: 6 points

Schreiben 5C

Waagerecht		Senkrecht	
4	wasche	1	Hausaufgaben
6	treffe	2	Uhr
7	machst	3	Viertel
9	Geburtstag	5	beginnt
12	esse	8	Schule
13	neun	10	stehe
14	fern	11	gehe

NATIONAL CURRICULUM LEVEL 2 (and AT3 Level 2) Total: 15 points

6 *Wie schmeckt's?*

Hören 6A

1E, 2B, 3D, 4A, 5F, 6C

NATIONAL CURRICULUM LEVEL 1 Total: 6 points

Hören 6B

1 Mittagessen
2 Frühstück
3 Abendessen
4 Frühstück
5 Abendessen
6 Mittagessen

NATIONAL CURRICULUM LEVELS 2, 3 (and AT3 Level 1) Total: 6 points

Hören 6C

See table below.

NATIONAL CURRICULUM LEVEL 3 (and AT3 Level 1) Total: 18 points

Hören 6D

Johannes: F, D
Katja: E, F, G, H, C, J, B, I

NATIONAL CURRICULUM LEVEL 3 Total: 10 points

Sprechen 6A

1 Orangensaft
2 Wurst
3 Brötchen
4 Marmelade
5 Honig
6 Milch
7 Butter
8 Käse
9 Tee
10 Kaffee

NATIONAL CURRICULUM LEVEL 1 Total: 10 points

Sprechen 6B

1 **A:** Was ißt und trinkst du zum Frühstück?
B: Ich esse Brötchen und Marmelade, und ich trinke Kaffee und Apfelsaft.
2 **A:** Was ißt und trinkst du zum Mittagessen?
B: Ich esse Hähnchen, Pommes frites und Salat, und ich trinke Cola.
3 **A:** Was ißt und trinkst du zum Abendessen?
B: Ich esse Brot, Schinken und Käse, und ich trinke Milch.
4 **A:** Was ißt und trinkst du zum Abendessen?
B: Ich esse Wurst, Brötchen und Eier, und ich trinke Limonade.
5 **A:** Was ißt und trinkst du zum Mittagessen?
B: Ich esse Salat, Frikadellen und Nudeln, und ich trinke Limonade.
6 **A:** Was ißt und trinkst du zum Frühstück?
B: Ich esse Toast mit Honig, und ich trinke Tee und Orangensaft.

NATIONAL CURRICULUM LEVEL 2
Total: 4 points per dialogue (B role only)

	Brötchen	Käse	Eier	Marmelade	Kaffee	Tee	Apfelsaft	Orangensaft
Nicole			✗		✔			✔
Lukas	✔			✔	✗		✔	
Petra			✔			✔		
Carmen	✔	✔		✗				
Bruno					✔	✔		✗
Karl	✔	✗		✔				

Sprechen 6C

1 **A:** Was ißt du gern?
B: Ich esse gern Pommes frites.
A: Was trinkst du gern?
B: Ich trinke gern Orangensaft.
A: Was ißt du nicht gern?
B: Ich esse nicht gern Eier.
A: Was trinkst du nicht gern?
B: Ich trinke nicht gern Tee.

2 **A:** Was ißt du gerne?
B: Ich esse gern Käse.
A: Was trinkst du gern?
B: Ich trinke gern Kaffee.
A: Was ißt du nicht gerne?
B: Ich esse nicht gerne Wurst.
A: Was trinkst du nicht gerne?
B: Ich trinke nicht gern Milch.

3 **A:** Was ißt du gern?
B: Ich esse gern Brötchen.
A: Was trinkst du gern?
B: Ich trinke gerne Kakao.
A: Was ißt du nicht gerne?
B: Ich esse nicht gerne Honig.
A: Was trinkst du nicht gern?
B: Ich trinke nicht gerne Apfelsaft.

4 **A:** Was ißt du gerne?
B: Ich esse gerne Schinken.
A: Was trinkst du gerne?
B: Ich trinke gerne Cola.
A: Was ißt du nicht gerne?
B: Ich esse nicht gerne Brot.
A: Was trinkst du nicht gerne?
B: Ich trinke nicht gerne Limonade.

5 **A:** Was ißt du gern?
B: Ich esse gerne Frikadellen.
A: Was trinkst du gern?
B: Ich trinke gern Milch.
A: Was ißt du nicht gerne?
B: Ich esse nicht gerne Marmelade.
A: Was trinkst du nicht gern?
B: Ich trinke nicht gerne Kaffee.

6 **A:** Was ißt du gerne?
B: Ich esse gerne Hähnchen.
A: Was trinkst du gern?
B: Ich trinke gern Apfelsaft.
A: Was ißt du nicht gerne?
B: Ich esse nicht gerne Salat.
A: Was trinkst du nicht gern?
B: Ich trinke nicht gern Orangensaft.

NATIONAL CURRICULUM LEVEL 3
(and AT1 Level 2) Total: 4 points per dialogue (B role only)

Sprechen 6D

Beispiel
Zum Frühstück esse ich gern Müsli.
Ich trinke gern Kaffee.
Ich esse nicht gern Toast.
Ich trinke nicht gern Tee.
Zum Mittagessen esse ich gern Pommes frites.
Ich trinke gern Cola.
Ich esse nicht gern Wurst.
Ich trinke nicht gern Apfelsaft.
Zum Abendessen esse ich gern Käse.
Ich trinke gern Milch.
Ich esse nicht gern Schinken.
Ich trinke nicht gern Orangensaft.

NATIONAL CURRICULUM LEVEL 3
Total: 4 points per meal

Lesen 6A

Kaffee – F
Apfelsaft – A
Kakao – E
Brötchen – J
Käse – H
Schinken – B
Eier – I
Wurst – C
Nudeln – D
Marmelade – G

NATIONAL CURRICULUM LEVEL 1 Total: 10 points

Lesen 6B

A3, B6, C2, D4, E1, F5

NATIONAL CURRICULUM LEVEL 2 Total: 6 points

Lesen 6C

1B, 2F, 3A, 4E, 5C, 6D

NATIONAL CURRICULUM LEVEL 2 Total: 6 points

Lesen 6D

Description 3

NATIONAL CURRICULUM LEVEL 3 Total: 1 point

Schreiben 6A

1 Tee
2 Orangensaft
3 Brötchen
4 Nudeln
5 Hähnchen
6 ein gekochtes Ei
7 Käse
8 Kaffee

NATIONAL CURRICULUM LEVEL 1 Total: 8 points

Schreiben 6B

1 Was trinkst du gern?
2 Ich esse nicht gern Hähnchen.
3 Ißt du gern Pommes frites?
4 Was trinkst du zum Frühstück?
5 Ich trinke nicht gern Kaffee.
6 Ich esse gern ein gekochtes Ei.

NATIONAL CURRICULUM LEVEL 2 Total: 6 points
(and AT3 Level 1)

Schreiben 6C

1 Ich esse gern *(any suitable lunch food items)*.
2 Ich esse nicht gern *(any disliked food)*.
3 Ich trinke gern *(any liked drinks)*.
4 Ich trinke nicht gern *(any disliked drinks)*.

NATIONAL CURRICULUM LEVEL 3 Total: 4 points
(and AT3 Level 2)

7 Schule

Hören 7A

1 ✔ 2 ✔ 3 ✗ 4 ✗ 5 ✗ 6 ✔ 7 ✗ 8 ✔ 9 ✗

NATIONAL CURRICULUM LEVEL 1 Total: 9 points

Hören 7B

1 2.00–4.00
2 5.15–6.15
3 7.15–8.45
4 3.00–4.30
5 2.30–3.30

NATIONAL CURRICULUM LEVEL 2 Total: 5 points

Hören 7C

1a, 2c, 3a, 4c, 5b, 6a, 7b, 8c

NATIONAL CURRICULUM LEVEL 3 TOTAL: 8 points

Sprechen 7A

1 Biologie 2 Deutsch 3 Musik 4 Mathe 5 Kunst
6 Chemie 7 Englisch 8 Geschichte 9 Erdkunde

NATIONAL CURRICULUM LEVEL 1 Total: 9 points

Sprechen 7B

1 Englisch, Spanisch und Französisch
2 Biologie und Chemie
3 Physik, Musik, Mathematik
4 Maria Richter lernt Geschichte.

NATIONAL CURRICULUM LEVEL 1
(and AT1 Level 1) Total: 12 points (three points each for nos. 1 & 3, two for no. 2, four for no. 4)

Sprechen 7C

Beispiele
1 Englisch gefällt mir – es ist interessant.
2 Deutsch ist ganz interessant.
3 Mein Lieblingsfach ist Kunst – es ist toll.
4 Sport gefällt mir – ich spiele gern Fußball.
5 Latein gefällt mir nicht – es ist langweilig!
(Any appropriate answers acceptable.)

NATIONAL CURRICULUM LEVELS 1, 2
(and AT3 Level 2) Total: 5 points

Sprechen 7D

Beispiel
A: Was hast du in der ersten Stunde?
B: Erdkunde.
A: Wie findest du Erdkunde?
B: Es ist toll!
B: Was hast du in der zweiten Stunde?
A: Mathe.
B: Wie findest du Mathe?
A: Es ist langweilig.
(Any appropriate dialogues acceptable.)

NATIONAL CURRICULUM LEVELS 2, 3, 4
(and AT1 Level 2)
Total: 8 points (2 points per dialogue for the first 4 dialogues)

Lesen 7A

1 Deutsch 2 Kunst 3 Geschichte 4 Chemie
5 Erdkunde 6 Werken

NATIONAL CURRICULUM LEVEL 1 Total: 6 points

Lesen 7B

Deutsch	Englisch
die Aula	hall
die Bibliothek	library
das Büro	office
der Klassenlehrer/ die Klassenlehrerin	tutor
der Parkplatz	car park
der Schüler/ die Schülerin	pupil
der Taschenrechner	(pocket) calculator
das Turnen	gym(nastics)

NATIONAL CURRICULUM LEVELS 2, 3 Total: 8 points

Lesen 7C

Dienstag, Mittwoch und *Donnerstag*
... Kunst. Das gefällt mir *nicht*.
Dann habe ich *Spanisch*.
... in der ersten Stunde *(Geschichte)*
... in den *dritten* und vierten Stunden
... *Physik* in der fünften Stunde

NATIONAL CURRICULUM LEVEL 4 Total: 6 points

Schreiben 7A

1 Montag 2 Mittwoch 3 Sonntag 4 Freitag
5 Samstag 6 Donnerstag 7 Dienstag

NATIONAL CURRICULUM LEVEL 1 Total: 7 points

Schreiben 7B

1 Wie *findest* du Deutsch?
2 Welches *Fach* gefällt dir nicht?
3 Ich habe Sport in der sechsten *Stunde*.
4 Sport ist mein *Lieblingsfach*.
5 Was *hast* du heute auf?
6 Wann machst du deine *Hausaufgaben/Schulaufgaben*?

NATIONAL CURRICULUM LEVELS 2 Total: 6 points
(and AT3 Level 2)

Schreiben 7C

(Any six sentences about subject preferences and times, e.g.:)
Sport gefällt mir. Das habe ich am Montag in der ersten Stunde.
Am Montag in der zweiten Stunde habe ich Kunst. Das gefällt mir nicht. *etc.*

NATIONAL CURRICULUM LEVELS 3, 4 Total: 6 points

8 Meine Freizeit

Hören 8A

Irene – D
Murat – F
Nicole – B
Daniel – E
Karl – C
Miriam – A

NATIONAL CURRICULUM LEVEL 1 Total 6 points

Hören 8B

1D, 2A, 3E, 4C, 5F, 6B

NATIONAL CURRICULUM LEVEL 1 Total: 6 points

Hören 8C

Lindenstraße – 18:10
Eurocops – 17:55
Die Tiger von Kanha – 21:05
Nachbarn – 14:45
Sport aus aller Welt – 15:30
Guten Appetit – 13:45

NATIONAL CURRICULUM LEVEL 2 Total: 6 points

Hören 8D

See table below.
Tamara and Beate are the best matched pair.

NATIONAL CURRICULUM LEVEL 3
Total: 16 points (14 for grid, 2 for correct pair)

Sprechen 8A

1 Ich spiele Fußball.
2 Ich spiele Tennis.
3 Ich sehe fern.
4 Ich gehe mit dem Hund spazieren.
5 Ich gehe in die Disco.
6 Ich schwimme/Ich gehe schwimmen.
7 Ich lese.
8 Ich reite.

NATIONAL CURRICULUM LEVEL 1 Total: 8 points

Sprechen 8B

Beispiele

1 A: Wie findest du Musiksendungen?
B: Toll!
2 A: Wie findest du Trickfilme?
B: Doof!
3 A: Wie findest du Sportsendungen?
B: Interessant!
4 A: Wie findest du Natursendungen?
B: Super!
5 A: Wie findest du die Nachrichten?
B: Langweilig!
6 A: Wie findest du Filme?
B: Toll!

(Any appropriate responses to the questions are acceptable.)

NATIONAL CURRICULUM LEVELS 2, 3 (and AT1 Level 2)
Total: 6 points each (1 point per question or answer)

Sprechen 8C

Beispiel

Ich spiele gern Fußball in meiner Freizeit. Ich lese gern, ich spiele mit dem Computer, und ich höre gern Musik.
Am liebsten fahre ich rad, oder ich bummle in der Stadt.
Ich sehe ungefähr zehn Stunden pro Woche fern. Am liebsten sehe ich Filme und Serien. Ich sehe nicht gern Nachrichten – sie sind langweilig! Talkshows sind auch doof, aber Musiksendungen und Natursendungen sind interessant.
(Any appropriate answers to the questions in a continuous speech are acceptable.)

NATIONAL CURRICULUM LEVELS 3, 4 (and AT3 Level 2)
Total: 8 points (2 points for each question answered)

Lesen 8A

1 Klavier **2** toll **3** doof **4** lese **5** Werbung

NATIONAL CURRICULUM LEVEL 1 Total: 5 points

Lesen 8B

1A, 2D, 3F, 4B, 5E, 6C

NATIONAL CURRICULUM LEVEL 2 Total: 6 points

Lesen 8C

C, G, A, F, D, H, E

NATIONAL CURRICULUM LEVELS 2c, 3 Total: 7 points

	Cycling	Disco	Walking dog	Reading	Town	TV
Anna		✔		✔		
Jörg	✔				✔	
Tamara			✔			✔
Heike	✔					
Marek				✔	✔	
Gerd		✔				
Beate			✔			✔
Sven	✔		✔			

Lesen 8D

1C, 2F, 3B, 4E, 5A, 6D

NATIONAL CURRICULUM LEVEL 3 Total: 6 points

Schreiben 8A

1 Fußball **2** Rad **3** Briefmarken **4** Klavier
5 Trickfilme **6** spazieren

NATIONAL CURRICULUM LEVEL 1 Total: 6 points

Schreiben 8B

1 FERN **2** HÖRE **3** BUMMLE **4** REITE **5** ZWEI
6 SENDUNG **7** LIEBSTEN **8** TREFFE
9 = FREIZEIT

NATIONAL CURRICULUM LEVEL 2 Total: 9 points
(and AT3 Level 2)

Schreiben 8C

Beispiel
Ich heiße *(name)*. Ich bin *(age)* Jahre alt. Ich *(activity)* gern. Am liebsten *(favourite activity)*. Ich sehe gern/nicht gern fern *(+ statement about a type of programme)*.

NATIONAL CURRICULUM LEVELS 3, 4
(and AT3 Level 3) Total: 10 points (2 points per sentence)

9 *Was kostet das?*

Hören 9A

Hamburger – 4,90 DM.
Bratwurst – 3,10 DM.
Frikadelle – 2,80 DM.
Pommes frites – 1,90 DM.
Eis – 2,00 DM.

NATIONAL CURRICULUM LEVEL 1 Total: 6 points

Hören 9B

1 Cola **2** 2 × Pommes **3** Apfelsaft **4** 4,50 DM
5 8,00 DM **6** 2 × Erdbeereis

NATIONAL CURRICULUM LEVEL 2 Total: 6 points

Hören 9C

See table below.

NATIONAL CURRICULUM LEVELS 3 Total: 12 points

Sprechen 9A

1 Eine Mark und eine Mark neunundneunzig. Das macht zwei Mark neunundneunzig.
2 Vier Mark fünf und neunundneunzig Pfennig. Das macht fünf Mark und vier Pfennig.
3 Acht Mark zehn und drei Mark zwanzig. Das macht elf Mark dreißig.
4 Zweiundsiebzig Mark fünfzig und neun Mark fünfzehn. Das macht einundachtzig Mark fünfundsechzig.

NATIONAL CURRICULUM LEVEL 1
Total: 12 points (1 point per price)

Sprechen 9B

1 Ich möchte ein Zitroneneis, bitte.
2 Einmal Bratwurst und zwei Frikadellen, bitte.
3 Was macht das, bitte?
4 Ich spare für Turnschuhe.
5 Ich fahre mit Renates Riesenrad.

NATIONAL CURRICULUM LEVELS 1, 2 Total: 5 points
(and AT3 Level 2)

Sprechen 9C

Beispiele
1 Was kostet das?
2 Was nimmst du?
3 Wofür sparst du?
4 Wofür gibst du dein Geld aus?
5 Fährst du gern mit der Achterbahn?
(Any appropriate questions are acceptable.)

NATIONAL CURRICULUM LEVEL 2 Total: 5 points
(and AT3 Level 2)

Sprechen 9D

1 – Was nimmst du, Martin?
– Eine Cola und Pommes frites, bitte.
– Und ich nehme eine Bratwurst, eine Portion Pommes und eine Cola. Also, eine Bratwurst, zwei Portionen Pommes und zweimal Cola, bitte.
2 – Was nimmst du, Hella?
– Ein Eis und einen Apfelsaft, bitte.
– Und ich nehme ein Eis und eine Cola. Also, zweimal Eis, einen Apfelsaft und eine Cola, bitte.
3 – Was nimmst du, Friedrich?
– Eine Frikadelle, eine Portion Pommes und eine Limonade, bitte.
– Und ich nehme ein Schaschlik und Pommes. Also, eine Frikadelle, ein Schaschlik, zwei Portionen Pommes frites und eine Limonade, bitte.
4 – Was nimmst du, Dagmar?
– Einen Hamburger und eine Limo, bitte.
– Und ich nehme eine Wurst, ein Eis und einen Apfelsaft. Also einen Hamburger, eine Limo, eine Wurst, ein Eis und einen Apfelsaft.
5 – Was nimmst du, Hasan?
– Zweimal Eis und eine Cola, bitte.

	Cassettes/ CDs	Bicycle	Sweets/ snacks	Sports gear	Clothes	Fair	Mags/ books	Computer
save for	6	5		2	1	8		1
spend on	3		3		4, 7		3, 7	

– Und ich nehme eine Packung Chips und eine Cola. Also, zwei Eis, zweimal Cola und eine Packung Chips.

6 – Was nimmst du, Tara?
– Ein Butterbrot mit Käse und ein Schaschlik, bitte.
– Und ich nehme einen Hamburger und eine Packung Chips. Also, ein Butterbrot mit Käse, ein Schaschlik, einen Hamburger, und eine Packung Chips.

NATIONAL CURRICULUM LEVEL 3
(and AT1 Level 2) Total: 2 points each per dialogue
(students take it in turns to start dialogue)

Lesen 9A

1 AF **2** KE **3** JB **4** CL **5** HI **6** GD

NATIONAL CURRICULUM LEVEL 1 Total: 6 points

Lesen 9B

Ich kaufe mir Pommes frites – E
Ich spare für Kleider – F
Wofür gibst du dein Geld aus? – C
Ich kaufe mir Chips – A
Wofür sparst du? – D
Ich gebe mein Geld für Kleider aus – B

NATIONAL CURRICULUM LEVEL 2 Total: 6 points

Lesen 9C

F, C, H, E, B, A, G, D

NATIONAL CURRICULUM LEVEL 3 Total: 8 points

Lesen 9D

1 ✔ **2** ✗ **3** ✗ **4** ✔ **5** ✗ **6** ✗ **7** ✔ **8** ✗

NATIONAL CURRICULUM LEVEL 4 Total: 8 points

Schreiben 9A

1 Geld **2** Bücher **3** spare **4** Fährst
5 Autoscooter/Riesenrad **6** liebsten
7 Riesenrad/Autoscooter

NATIONAL CURRICULUM LEVEL 1 Total: 7 points
(and AT3 Level 2)

Schreiben 9B

1 KÄSE **2** POMMES FRITES **3** SCHASCHLIK
4 HAMBURGER **5** BRATWURST **6** FRIKADELLEN
7 SCHOKOLADE **8** = EISBUDE

NATIONAL CURRICULUM LEVEL 2 Total: 8 points

Schreiben 9C

Chips
Turnschuhe
Apfelsaft
Kassetten
Kleider
Cola

NATIONAL CURRICULUM
LEVEL 2 Total: 6 points

Schreiben 9D

1 Wofür sparst du?
2 Wofür gibst du dein Geld aus?
3 Ich gebe mein Geld für das Kino aus.
4 Ich spare für ein Rad.
5 Gehst du gern zum Jahrmarkt?
6 Am liebsten fahre ich mit der Achterbahn.
(Any appropriate sentences are acceptable.)

NATIONAL CURRICULUM LEVEL 3
Total: 12 points (2 points per sentence)

10 Wie schön!

Hören 10A

Berlin – sunny
London – cold
Paris – windy
Rom – snow
Lissabon – rain
Warschau – foggy
Athen – hot

NATIONAL CURRICULUM LEVEL 1 Total: 7 points

Hören 10B

1 Christiana – school
2 Achim – pets
3 Sophia – food
4 Fatima – house & garden
5 Hans-Peter – hobbies
6 Jörg – TV

NATIONAL CURRICULUM LEVEL 2 Total: 6 points

Hören 10C

See table below.

NATIONAL CURRICULUM LEVEL 3 Total: 12 points

Hören 10D

D, B, H, A, L, C, F, I

NATIONAL CURRICULUM LEVEL 4 Total: 8 points

Sprechen 10A

1 Die Sonne scheint.
2 Es regnet.
3 Es ist windig.

	Sea	Country	Mountains	Hotel	Holiday house	Youth hostel	Tent
Barbara	✔			✔			
Ines		✔				✔	
Stefan			✔	✔			
Joachim		✔					✔
Elisabeth			✔		✔		
Hermann	✔						✔

4 Es ist neblig.
5 Es ist heiß.
6 Es ist kalt.
7 Es schneit.

NATIONAL CURRICULUM LEVEL 2 Total: 7 points

Sprechen 10B

1 **A:** Was machst du im Sommer?
B: Ich fahre aufs Land. Ich wohne in einem Zelt.
2 **A:** Was machst du im Sommer?
B: Ich fahre ins Gebirge. Ich wohne in einer Jugendherberge.
3 **A:** Was machst du im Sommer?
B: Ich fahre an die See. Ich wohne in einem Hotel.
4 **A:** Was machst du im Sommer?
B: Ich fahre nicht weg. Ich bleibe zu Hause.
5 **A:** Was machst du im Sommer?
B: Ich fahre ins Gebirge. Ich wohne in einem Ferienhaus.
6 **A:** Was machst du im Sommer?
B: Ich fahre ans Meer. Ich wohne in einem Zelt.

NATIONAL CURRICULUM LEVEL 2
Total: 9 points each (1 point per question/statement: students take it in turns to start dialogue.)

Sprechen 10C

1 **B:** Wohin fährst du?
A: Ich fahre aufs Land.
B: Mit wem fährst du?
A: Ich fahre mit meiner Familie.
B: Wie lange bleibst du?
A: Zwei Wochen.
B: Was machst du?
A: Ich fahre rad, ich lese und ich sehe fern.
2 **A:** Wohin fährst du?
B: Ich fahre an die See.
A: Mit wem fährst du?
B: Ich fahre alleine.
A: Wie lange bleibst du?
B: Eine Woche.
A: Was machst du?
B: Ich schwimme, ich spiele Tennis, und ich gehe in die Disco.

NATIONAL CURRICULUM LEVEL 4 Total: 8 points each
(and AT1 Level 2)

Sprechen 10D

Beispiel
Ich fahre am liebsten nach Frankreich. Ich fahre mit meiner Familie ans Meer. Wir wohnen zwei Wochen dort in einem Ferienhaus. Das Wetter ist sehr schön – die Sonne scheint, und es ist sehr warm.
Ich schwimme, ich fahre rad, und ich spiele Fußball und Tennis. Ich bummle auch in der Stadt. Abends lese ich, oder ich sehe fern.

NATIONAL CURRICULUM LEVEL 4
Total: 8 points (2 points each for any 4 relevant pieces of information)

Lesen 10A

1F, 2D, 3A, 4E, 5G, 6C, 7B

NATIONAL CURRICULUM LEVEL 2 Total: 7 points

Lesen 10B

Deutsch	**Englisch**
Regenbogen	rainbow
Regenmantel	raincoat, mac
Regenschirm	umbrella
Schneemann	snowman
Sonnenbrand	sunburn
Windhund	greyhound
Windmühle	windmill
Windschutzscheibe	windscreen

NATIONAL CURRICULUM LEVELS 2, 3 Total: 8 points

Lesen 10C

1C, 2F, 3D, 4A, 5B, 6E

NATIONAL CURRICULUM LEVEL 3 Total: 6 points

Lesen 10D

Wants to know what you are doing in the summer.
Can you go to Italy?
Leaving for Rimini/on 25th July/with her family.
Staying in a little holiday house/by the sea.
Go swimming/every day/or cycling/in the country.
Sister not going this year/because she is camping/in Austria/with friends.
You can have her bedroom.

NATIONAL CURRICULUM LEVEL 4
Total: 10 points (for any 10 pieces of information)

Schreiben 10A

1 Wie ist das *Wetter*?
2 Die Sonne *scheint*.
3 Wohin *fährst* du?
4 Ich fahre nach *Deutschland*.
5 Wir wohnen in einem *Ferienhaus*.
6 Es *schneit*.

NATIONAL CURRICULUM LEVELS 1, 2 Total: 6 points
(and AT3 Level 2)

Schreiben 10B

1 Hotel **2** Zelt **3** Jugendherberge **4** Gebirge
5 Land **6** Schule

NATIONAL CURRICULUM LEVEL 2 Total: 6 points

Schreiben 10C

1 Wie ist das Wetter?
2 Wohin fährst du?
3 Mit wem fährst du?
4 Wie lange bleibst du?
5 Wo wohnst du?
6 Was machst du?
(Any appropriate questions are acceptable.)

NATIONAL CURRICULUM LEVEL 3
(and AT3 Level 2) Total: 12 points (2 points per question)

Schreiben 10D

(Minimum of three sentences covering activity/activities, weather and holiday plans.)

NATIONAL CURRICULUM LEVEL 4
(and AT3 Level 3) Total: 6 points (2 points per sentence)

Abschlußtest (Kapitel 1–10)

Hören 1–10A

1A, 2D, 3F, 4C, 5B, 6E

NATIONAL CURRICULUM LEVEL 1 Total: 6 points

Hören 1–10B

29, 54, 12, 68, 45, 30, 86, 92, 47, 13, 21, 74

NATIONAL CURRICULUM LEVEL 1 Total: 12 points

Hören 1–10C

	Name	Wohnort	Familie	Haustiere	Hobbys
1	Dieter	✔			
2	Susi			✔	
3	Alexandra		✔		
4	Yusuf				✔
5	Nicole	✔			

NATIONAL CURRICULUM LEVEL 2 Total: 5 points

Hören 1–10D

1E, 2D, 3B, 4A, 5F, 6C

NATIONAL CURRICULUM LEVEL 2 Total: 6 points

Hören 1–10E

1C, 2F, 3D, 4A, 5E, 6B

NATIONAL CURRICULUM LEVEL 3 Total: 6 points
(and AT3 Level 2)

Hören 1–10F

(The following details should be circled:)

Peter
Maier
13
17.6.
Mozartstraße 45, Neu-Ulm,
94 32 68

NATIONAL CURRICULUM LEVEL 3 Total: 8 points

Sprechen 1–10A

1 Ein Kuli
2 Cola
3 Geld
4 Ein Lineal
5 Ein Heft
6 Schokolade
7 Kassetten
8 Turnschuhe
9 Ein Buch

NATIONAL CURRICULUM LEVEL 1 Total: 9 points

Sprechen 1–10B

1 Dirk: D-I-R-K
2 Pawel: P-A-W-E-L
3 Josefa: J-O-S-E-F-A
4 Micha: M-I-C-H-A
5 Birgit: B-I-R-G-I-T
6 Vera: V-E-R-A

NATIONAL CURRICULUM LEVEL 2 Total: 30 points

Sprechen 1–10C

A: Wie heißt du?
B: Ich heiße Kirsten Pfeifer. Und du?
A: Ich heiße Peter Müller.
B: Wie alt bist du?
A: Ich bin dreizehn Jahre alt. Wie alt bist du?
B: Ich bin zwölf.
A: Wo wohnst du?
B: Ich wohne in Schwerin. Wo wohnst du?
A: In Mannheim.
B: Hast du Geschwister?
A: Ja, ich habe einen Bruder. Hast du Geschwister?
B: Ja, ich habe eine Schwester.

NATIONAL CURRICULUM LEVELS 3, 4 (and AT1 Level 2)
Total: 8 points each (1 point per question/response)

Sprechen 1–10D

Beispiel

A: Wie heißt du?
B: Ich heiße Samuela.
A: Hast du Geschwister?
B: Ja, ich habe zwei Brüder und eine Schwester.
A: Hast du Haustiere?
B: Ich habe einen Hund.
A: Was ißt du gern?
B: Ich esse gern Schaschlik und Pommes.
A: Was ist dein Lieblingsfach?
B: Chemie. Das ist interessant.
A: Was machst du am liebsten in deiner Freizeit?
B: Ich lese, und ich schwimme.
A: Wofür gibst du dein Geld aus?
B: Ich gebe mein Geld für Bücher aus.
A: Wohin fährst du im Sommer?
B: Ich fahre mit meiner Familie ans Meer.
(Any appropriate questions/answers are acceptable.)

NATIONAL CURRICULUM LEVELS 4, 5 (and AT1 Level 2)
Total: 16 points each (1 point per question/response)

Sprechen 1–10E

Beispiel

4 Mein Stundenplan und Hausaufgaben (Montags)
Am Montag in der ersten Stunde habe ich Geschichte. Das geht. In der zweiten und dritten Stunden habe ich Sport. Das ist toll! Sport ist mein Lieblingsfach. In der vierten Stunde habe ich Deutsch. Das gefällt mir, aber in der fünften Stunde habe ich Erdkunde. Das gefällt mir nicht – es ist langweilig!
Ich mache meine Hausaufgaben zwischen fünf und halb

sieben. Montag mache ich Geschichte, Deutsch und Erdkunde.
(Any appropriate response is acceptable.)

NATIONAL CURRICULUM LEVEL 4 (and AT3 Level 1)
Total: 12 points (2 points each for any 6 sentences)

Lesen 1–10A

Schaschlik – kebab
Chips – crisps
Pommes frites – chips
Wurst – sausage
Apfelsaft – apple juice
Cola – Coca-Cola
Milch – milk
Kakao – cocoa
Limo – lemonade
Frikadelle – meat ball

NATIONAL CURRICULUM LEVEL 1 Total: 10 points

Lesen 1–10B

A3, B6, C1, D4, E5, F2

NATIONAL CURRICULUM LEVEL 2 Total: 6 points

Lesen 1–10C

Deutsch	**Englisch**
der Neffe	nephew
der Wolkenkratzer	sky scraper
der Dackel	dachshund
der Hagel	hail
das Schach	chess
das Geschenk	present
der Kuchen	cake
das Hallenbad	(indoor) swimming pool

NATIONAL CURRICULUM LEVELS 2, 3 Total: 8 points

Lesen 1–10D

5, 3, 1, 6, 4, 2

NATIONAL CURRICULUM LEVEL 2 Total: 6 points

Lesen 1–10E

1 ✗ **2** ✗ **3** ✔ **4** ✗ **5** ✔

NATIONAL CURRICULUM LEVEL 3 Total: 5 points

Lesen 1–10F

A3, B8, C6, D1, E4, F7, G2, H5

NATIONAL CURRICULUM LEVEL 3 Total: 8 points

Lesen 1–10G

A7, B3, C6, D4, E9, F8, G1, H5, I2

NATIONAL CURRICULUM LEVEL 5 Total: 9 points

Schreiben 1–10A

1 der Tisch **2** das Bett **3** die Turnschuhe
4 der Hund **5** der Goldfisch **6** das Heft **7** der Kuli
8 die Bücher

NATIONAL CURRICULUM LEVEL 1 Total: 8 points

Schreiben 1–10B

1 heißt
2 in der Stadtmitte?
3 Spielst du gern
4 Was ißt du
5 dein Lieblingsfach?
6 in deiner Freizeit?

NATIONAL CURRICULUM LEVEL 2 Total: 6 points
(and AT3 Level 2)

Schreiben 1–10C

1 Ich heiße Jo.
2 Wie alt bist du?
3 Ich habe einen Bruder.
4 Ich trinke gern Apfelsaft.
5 Wie spät ist es?
6 Mein Lieblingsfach ist Geschichte.

NATIONAL CURRICULUM LEVEL 2 Total: 6 points
(and AT3 Level 1)

Schreiben 1–10D

1 Kaffee **2** Katze **3** Wohnung **4** Briefmarken
5 fünf **6** Chips **7** Deutschland **8** Erdkunde
9 Lineal **10** Kaninchen

NATIONAL CURRICULUM LEVEL 2 Total: 10 points

Schreiben 1–10E

1 Es ist windig.
2 Es regnet.
3 Die Sonne scheint.
4 Es schneit.
5 Es ist neblig.
6 Es ist heiß.
7 Es ist kalt.

NATIONAL CURRICULUM LEVEL 3 Total: 7 points

Schreiben 1–10F

1 Wie heißt du?
2 Hast du ein Haustier?
3 Was machst du an deinem Geburtstag?
4 Was hast du in der ersten Stunde?
5 Wofür sparst du?
6 Wohin fährst du/Was machst du im Sommer?
(Any appropriate question is acceptable.)

NATIONAL CURRICULUM LEVEL 3 Total: 6 points

Schreiben 1–10G

(Degree of detail will determine the National Curriculum Level. Students need to provide accurate detail in all 4 categories listed.)

NATIONAL CURRICULUM LEVELS 4, 5
Total: 12 points (3 points per category)